# PASSAGES FOR
# RUSSIAN TRANSLATION AND COMPREHENSION

SBN 569-07481-9

# PREFACE

It is hoped that the first part of this book will meet a need which has been felt by some teachers of Russian in this country, and give them a selection of passages suitable for translation into Russian by students after a year to a year and a half's work at the language. The authors are well aware that vocabulary at this stage is bound to be rather limited, and therefore anything in the nature of a selection of passages from standard English authors would present difficulties of vocabulary too great for such students.

The second part consists of a number of Comprehension Tests; of these some have been specially written, others are simple tales by Tolstoy. They have been divided into sections of a convenient length, and a selection of questions has been added to each. It is suggested that these questions should be used for both oral and written work, and it is further suggested that the teacher might well elaborate on them and make up similar ones. The essential thing is that by constant repetition of questions and answers in different ways, the student may be enabled to enlarge his or her own vocabulary and be led to feel that some real acquaintance with the living language is being gained.

A. S. M.
N. W.

London, 1947

# CONTENTS

# PASSAGES FOR RUSSIAN TRANSLATION AND COMPREHENSION

By

## A. S. MACPHERSON, M.A.

and

## N. WISSOTZKY

(PUBLISHERS) LTD.
LONDON AND WELLINGBOROUGH, 1972

# TRANSLATION PIECES

## (English-Russian)

### 1

### A FAMILY

Peter Ivanov and his family live in a small house not far from the university.  The father is a professor and works at the university ;  they have two children, a son and a daughter. The boy goes to school each day, but the girl is still too small.  Behind their house is a garden in which the father works and the children often play.  In the garden are flowers and vegetables, and the family is very fond of sitting or working in it.  When the weather is warm enough they spend many hours there.

In the summer they go into the country and stay there for two or three weeks.  Are you fond of the country ?

*Notes*

two children : двóе детéй
for two or three weeks : omit ' for '

### 2

### WINTER

The trees are all bare and winter has come.  The snow covers everything with a white mantle :  the fields, the streets, the roofs of the houses.  The rivers and lakes are frozen over, and people are able to skate.  The children too are glad, because they are fond of playing in the snow ;  they can make snowballs and snowmen and go tobogganing.

Katya and her brothers have made a very big snowman in the field opposite their house; its eyes are two pieces of coal, and it has a pipe in its mouth.

But when spring comes and the weather becomes warmer, the snowman will melt in the sun.

In spring the trees will soon be covered with green leaves; flowers will appear, and Katya's father will work a great deal in the garden.

*Notes*

    in the snow : в снегу́
    when spring comes : fut. perfective of прийти́
    in its mouth : во рту
    in the sun : на со́лнце

# 8

# LETTERS

Each morning the postman brings us our letters; generally there are several letters for my parents, and sometimes I get a letter or a post card from a friend or one of our relations. But July 31st is my birthday, and then I always get a lot of letters and sometimes three or four parcels. Last year I got six books, a stamp-album and a new camera.

One of the letters I received had come from Russia; my uncle went to the Soviet Union two years ago and is working in a big office in Leningrad.

I hope to learn Russian some day; some of the boys at our school are learning it, and although it is not an easy language, they like their lessons and are making progress.

*Notes*

    there are : быва́ет
    July 31st : genitive case
    learn Russian some day : вы́учиться ру́сскому языку́ когда́-нибудь
    some of : не́которые из

## 4

## OUR HOUSE

We live in a new house in a quiet suburb.  In the house there are seven rooms, a kitchen and a bathroom.  The sitting-room looks out on to the street, where buses and cars go to and fro and people go past the house to the shops.  The kitchen is very light and convenient, and my wife is very proud of it and is very fond of working there.  We have made one of the rooms upstairs into a nursery where the children can play.  There has been a lot of work in the garden: we have planted a few fruit trees, have made a lawn and flower-beds.  This year we have also grown our own vegetables.  Unfortunately our neighbours' cat comes into the garden rather often and breaks the plants.  But the children are very fond of it and beg me not to drive it away.

*Notes*

 in a quiet suburb: на + prepositional
 made into a nursery: сделали детской
 to grow (vegetables): посадить

## 5

## A LITTLE RUSSIAN GIRL

Sonya is a little girl who lives in a small house in the country.  Her two brothers, Ivan and Peter, are older than she is, and she has no sisters.  She and her brothers go to school every day, but to-day she has a cold and so must stay at home, and she is lonely without them.

While she is playing with her toys in the dining-room, she looks out of the window and sees the cat who is trying to catch a bird, but the bird flies away quickly, and Sonya is very glad.

At 12 o'clock her mother, who has been shopping in the town, comes back and gives her a parcel.  Sonya undoes it as quickly as she can and finds that it contains a beautiful new doll.   Her mother says:  I saw this doll in the toy-shop and bought it for you, as you cannot go out with Ivan and Peter to-day.

*Notes*

> while : here = when
> as quickly as she can : как мо́жно скоре́е
> go out : вы́йти гуля́ть

# 6

## AT HOME

Young Alexei is sitting at the table and reading a book. He is very fond of reading, and sometimes when his brothers and sisters are playing in the garden, he prefers to sit at home and read.   To-day he is enjoying a book which his mother bought him a few days ago and which is called *Tales by Tolstoy*.

But here comes his mother into the room in order to lay the table for dinner.   " Alyosha," she says, " stop reading now ; I want to lay the table, and you can help me."   Soon everything is ready ;  the other children come in from the garden, and they and their mother sit down to table.   First they have soup, then meat with vegetables, and after that, cheese or fruit.

After dinner the children clear the table and carry the crockery into the kitchen; half an hour later they a.l go with their mother to the park.

*Notes*

> at the table : за + instrumental
> enjoying : reading with pleasure
> by Tolstoy : gen. of Толсто́й
> here : вот
> for (dinner) : для
> stop reading : переста́нь чита́ть
> (sit down) to table : за + accusative
> have (soup, etc.) : eat
> after that : по́сле э́того

# 7

## A DAY IN TOWN

Yesterday I had to go to town. When I left the house it was raining, and so I put on a macintosh and took an umbrella. I do not like umbrellas, but when I go to town I generally take one.

I walked to the station and then got into a train which left at 11.15 and arrived in town at 12.0. Although the train was crowded, I found a seat and was able to read my newspaper. When we left the Central Station, the weather was fine.

I had soon finished my business, and as the sun was shining brightly, I went into the big park and sat there for nearly an hour. As I was walking by the lake, I met our doctor and his wife. We began discussing Shostakovitch's new symphony and modern music in general. As it was getting late, they invited me to go and have supper with them; I spent a very pleasant evening with them.

*Notes*

take (umbrella, etc.): брать
one: say, umbrella
walked: пошёл
get into train: сесть на поезд
for nearly an hour: omit ' for '
by (the lake): вдоль + genitive
go and have supper with them: пойти к ним поужинать

# 8

## A YOUNG ENGLISHMAN IN MOSCOW

Last month John received a telegram from Moscow, and a few days later he went there, as he had been given a job in a big factory.   He has not very much free time, but from time to time he is able to go to a concert, a theatre or a lecture ;  he is also still having Russian lessons.   When he left England he could read Russian fairly well, and understood people if they spoke slowly.   He is very anxious to see Leningrad, and hopes this will be possible in the summer.

He has made friends with some Russian people, and I hope they will invite him to their homes, so that he may get to know Russian life.   On Sundays he goes to a Russian church, and although he does not always understand everything he hears, he likes listening to the service.

*Notes*

 from Moscow : из М.
 he had been given : say, had received
 in a factory : на + prepositional
 have Russian lessons : учиться русскому языку
 he is anxious : ему очень хочется
 Russian people : omit ' people '
 invite to their homes : приглашать к себе
 so that he may : чтобы он мог
 on Sundays : по воскресеньям

## 9

# WHAT I SHALL DO TO-DAY

It is already seven o'clock; I must get up. It is very cold in the room, and I am very warm and comfortable in bed. I do not like getting up early in the morning in winter when it is dark and cold. But all the same it is time to get up, or I shall be late at the office. I see it is raining, so I must not forget to take my umbrella.

This evening my wife and I have decided to go to the theatre; she will call for me at the office and we shall go there together. Yesterday after work I went to the theatre for tickets. When I arrived there, a lot of people were standing in front of the theatre; but although I had to wait nearly half an hour, I succeeded in getting two good seats. We are going to see Moussorgsky's opera *Boris Godunov*, which we have never seen yet, but we hear that the performance is very good.

*Notes*

in the room : begin sentence with this
for (tickets) : за + instrumental (idea of fetching)
arrived there : arrived thither
a lot of people : мно́го наро́ду, followed by neuter verb
I had to : мне пришло́сь + infinitive
we hear that : говоря́т, что

## 10

## I AM FOND OF BUYING BOOKS

Last week my uncle gave me some money and said : " Now you can buy yourself some more books." He knows that I am very fond of books. So this morning I went to the old bookshop in the lane near the cathedral. Do you know it? I very often go there, because it is always possible to find interesting books there which are not too expensive. I saw very many books there to-day, and for a long time I could not decide which to buy. In the end I bought Turgenev's *Fathers and Sons*, and also a book of English stories. I have been learning English for three years and am very glad that I can read an English story if it is not too difficult. Of course I have to use a dictionary from time to time, but I do not use it as often as I did a year ago. During this winter I have made the acquaintance of a young Englishman with whom I talk English each week. He has invited me to go to England next year, and I very much hope that this will be possible.

*Notes*

 yourself : себе
 to find : perfective
 Fathers and Sons : Отцы́ и Де́ти
 (book) of English stories : (кни́га) с + instrumental
 I have been learning English, etc. : say, I already three years am
  learning
 during this winter : э́той зимо́й
 each week : accusative
 very much (hope) : о́чень

## 11

# LIFE  IN  A  BIG  TOWN

To walk along the streets of a big town is always interesting and sometimes amusing. Early in the morning men and women hurry to their offices, shops or factories, and the children run to school. After this women come into the town to do their shopping; in the windows of the shops they see a lot of attractive things, and they stand for a long time in front of them, discussing what they shall buy.

The street is crowded with buses, trams, motor-cars, lorries, carts and bicycles; all is full of movement and life. I find it interesting to look at the faces of the passers-by, and I try to imagine what they do and what sort of people they are

In a big town there are always a good many cinemas, and many people go to the cinema at least once a week. Besides the cinemas there is generally a theatre, and sometimes a concert-hall. I am very fond of music and go to a good concert as often as possible. Which do you prefer: concerts, films, or the theatre?

*Notes*

to do their shopping: за поку́пками
what they shall buy: что им купи́ть
find it interesting: omit ' it ' and put ' interesting ' into instrumental
look at the faces of passers-by: смотре́ть на ли́ца проходя́щих
what sort of people they are: что они́ за лю́ди
once a week: раз в неде́лю
there is generally: обыкнове́нно быва́ет
as often as possible: как мо́жно ча́ще

## 12

# TWO FRIENDS MEET  (I)

*Anna Nikolaevna:* Good morning, Vera Petrovna.   If you are going into the town, I should like to come with you, as I must do some shopping.

*Vera Petrovna:* Certainly;  let us walk there and come back by bus, as it will be unpleasant to carry heavy baskets.

*A. N.:* It is a lovely morning;  I'm sure it won't rain.

*V. P.:* What are you going to buy?

*A N.:* Fruit and vegetables in the market, and some stamps at the post office.   I also need some new shoes.

*V. P.:*  I must buy some shirts for Ivan, some socks for Peter, and some handkerchiefs for my husband.

They walk to the town, and as they cross the bridge, Anna Nikolaevna says:  We will meet in an hour in front of the big church;  we can then go into the restaurant and have lunch.

*V. P.:* Very well, that's a good idea.

*Notes*

should like to come : хочу пойти
let us walk : пойдёмте пешком
it is a lovely morning : the morning is lovely
we will meet : N.B. reflexive
in an hour : через час
that's a good idea : отлично

## 13

## TWO FRIENDS MEET (II)

At 12 o'clock the two ladies meet and go to the restaurant. They sit down at a table near the window and order lunch.

*Anna Nikolaevna:* I hope you were able to buy what you wanted.

*Vera Petrovna:* Yes, I found everything, and also bought a pretty blue dress for Natasha. Did you succeed in getting your shoes?

*A. N.:* Yes, I found just what I wanted. By the way, do you remember Olga Ivanovna who used to live in the house at the corner of London Street?

*V. P.:* Of course. I was very fond of her, but I haven't seen her for many years.

*A. N.:* She has been abroad, but has now returned home, and I met her in the market this morning. She is living in a flat near the theatre.

*V. P.:* I am very glad. I will write to her and ask when we can go and see her.

The two ladies finish their lunch and then go home by bus.

*Notes*

    just what I wanted : как раз то, что хотéла
    at the corner : на углу́
    London Street : Ло́ндонская у́лица
    for many years : omit ' for '
    go and see her : зайти́ к ней

## 14

## HE WAS NOT LISTENING

It is 8.55 a.m. and the pupils are already in the classroom. At 9 o'clock the teacher comes in and begins the lesson. To-day he reads a story to the class and then asks the pupils questions.  Nearly all the pupils answer well, but Peter cannot answer a single question.  While the teacher was reading the story, he was looking out of the window at a bird on a tree. In a moment it flew away and soon came back, carrying something in its beak.  "Oh," thought Peter, "it is building a nest."  He was so interested that he did not hear what the teacher was saying, and so when the teacher asked him a question, he could not answer.  The teacher was angry, and Peter had to stay in the classroom and work while the other pupils were playing out of doors.

*Notes*

    not a single question : ни один вопрос
    in (a moment): через
    carrying : она несла
    stay : say, sit

## 15

## I BUY A TIE

The day after to-morrow is my brother's birthday; I know that he needs a new tie, and so I have decided to give him one for a present.   When I went into a shop last Thursday, the assistant came up to me and asked what I wanted.   " Please show me some ties," I said, and he brought several and showed them to me.   But I did not like them, and I had to go into two more shops before I found one that pleased me.   I finally chose a blue one and asked how much it cost.   " 4 roubles," replied the assistant, so I gave him a note.   He took it, went away, and soon came back with the change and the tie;  I thanked him and went out of the shop.

As I had nothing to do after that, I went with my father to a restaurant near his office.   After lunch we both went to a cinema and saw two excellent films:  one showed scenes of Canada and its vast prairies, magnificent mountains and thick forests, and the second was a detective film. My father and I enjoyed the films very much, and we went home together in the evening.

*Notes*

for a present: в подáрок
came up to me: подошёл ко мне
what I wanted: что мне угóдно
please show me: say, show me please
one that (pleased me): то, что
two more: ещё два
came back with: came back and gave me
as I had nothing to do: так как мне нéчего бы́ло дéлать
enjoyed: use нрáвиться

## 16

## SERGEI TALKS ABOUT HIS FAMILY

*William:* Where do you live, Sergei?

*Sergei:* We live in Moscow.

*W.:* Moscow is a large and beautiful city, isn't it?

*S.:* Yes, and we are very proud that we live in the capital of the Soviet Union

*W.:* Have you any brothers or sisters?

*S.:* I have one brother and two sisters. They are all younger than I. My brother goes to school, but the two girls are still too small.

*W.:* Does your father work in Moscow?

*S.:* Yes, he works in a big office there; but he often goes to Leningrad and other big cities on business.

*W.:* What will you do when you leave school?

*S.:* I want to work in the same firm as my father. Later I hope they will send me to England, as we have friends there, and I want to learn to speak English well. We have English lessons at school, and I like the language very much; our teacher says I have a good pronunciation.

*W.:* I wish you good luck. Good-bye.

*Notes*

you: 2nd singular throughout
isn't it?: не пра́вда ли?
the two girls: об́е де́вочки
on business: по дела́м
leave (school): future perfective of конча́ть
later: впосле́дствии
good luck: всего́ хоро́шего

# 17

## AN UNPLEASANT ADVENTURE

One day two little girls went into the wood for mushrooms. When they were going home they had to cross the railway, and as they could not see any trains, they walked along the lines for a little while.  Suddenly, however, they heard the whistle of an engine, and the elder girl shouted to her sister, who was a little way in front, to stop.  But the train was already near, and because of its noise the little girl did not hear what her sister said.  She began to run, but dropped her basket.  The engine-driver saw her, but although he put on his brakes hard, he could not stop the train.

When the train had passed, the little girl was lying between the rails, very frightened, but unhurt.  Her sister at once ran up to her, put her arm round her, and helped her to get up. They picked up the mushrooms, put them into the basket, and then went home.

*Notes*

    for mushrooms: за + instrumental (idea of fetching)
    could not see any trains: не видели никакого поезда
    for a little while : некоторое время
    put on his brakes hard : затормозил изо всех сил
    unhurt : без всяких повреждений
    put her arm round her : обняла её

## 18

# A CHAT WITH THE FARMERS

A few days ago Nicholas was walking by the big lake not far from the town where he lives. It was a beautiful summer day, and on the lake there were many large and small boats. From time to time steamers went past, crowded with gay and noisy people. But although Nicholas is very fond of going by steamer, that day he preferred to walk.

When he came to the village of T. he went into the little inn, ordered a glass of beer and sat down at a table. There were several farmers in the inn, and Nicholas soon got into conversation with them. They told him about their work on the farms, about the cattle, and about the harvest, which is very good this year. Nicholas was very interested, for although he has to work in a big town, he is very fond of going into the country and chatting with the peasants. When it is possible, he will give up his work in the town and go to the Ukraine and work on a farm there.

*Notes*

 by (the lake): вдоль (gen.)
 went past: проходи́ли
 go by steamer: е́здить на парохо́де
 get into conversation with: разговори́ться с
 when it is possible: future

## 19

# A WET DAY

It is raining, and so we must stay at home.  Yesterday the weather was so lovely that we were able to spend the whole day in the open air, but to-day it is quite impossible to go out.  What shall we do?

Let us sit in the dining-room and work a bit.  I want to finish Tolstoy's *War and Peace*, and I must also write two letters:  one to my brother who is a doctor in a hospital in France, and another to a school-friend whom I have not seen for a long time.  For the last three years he has been living in the U.S.A. but will soon be returning to Europe.  I hope he will soon come here, for I know he will tell us a great deal about the U.S.A. and his life there.  At first it was difficult for him to find work, but in the end he succeeded. He travelled a lot, saw many of the big cities and got to know a good many people there, and was very happy in America. He will probably go back there next year.

*Notes*

what shall we do?: что нам де́лать?
let us sit: дава́йте ся́дем
whom I have not seen for a long time: кото́рого я давно́ не вида́л
for the last three years: после́дние три го́да
he has been living: present

## 20

## THE PEASANT AND HIS DONKEY

One day a peasant and his son were walking along the road and taking their donkey to a little town in order to sell him in the market.   Not far from their village they met a soldier who began to laugh at them, and said :  " Look at this man who walks along the dusty road, but his donkey carries nothing !  Why does he not ride on the donkey? "  When the peasant heard this, he got on the donkey ;  but after a few minutes another soldier met them and exclaimed :  " That peasant is very cruel ;  he rides comfortably on the donkey, but his poor little son has to walk."  So the peasant put his son in front of him on the saddle, and they both rode on the donkey.   Half an hour later two women saw them and said :  " What a cruel man !  He makes the donkey carry him and his son ;  it is disgraceful to treat an animal like that."  Then the peasant realised that it is impossible to follow every one's advice, and he decided to pay no attention to anyone.

*Notes*

 take : lead
 look at : perfective imperative
 ride : éхать
 got on : сел на + accusative
 put in front of him : посадил перед собой
 like that : таким образом
 anyone : here, no one

# 21

## AN UNEXPECTED VISITOR

Last Wednesday evening about 8.30 my wife and I were sitting comfortably in front of the fire ; she was doing needle-work, and I was smoking a cigarette and reading the news-paper. Suddenly we heard steps, and then someone knocked at the door and rang the bell ; our dog who was lying between us woke up and began to bark loudly. My wife said : " Who is that ? Visitors do not often come so late."

I got up from my arm-chair and went and opened the door, and to my amazement saw a very old school-friend. " John ! " I exclaimed, " I never thought that it was you ! Come in. and let me introduce you to my wife." He did not know my wife, of course, as I had married only quite recently. I had often spoken to her of him, and she was very glad to make his acquaintance. We spent the rest of the evening till midnight talking of all sorts of things, and as John left, my wife invited him to come back as soon as possible and stay with us for a few days.

*Notes*

begin to bark : залаять
someone knocked at the door : кто-то постучал в дверь
who is that ? : кто там ?
to my amazement : к моему удивлению
that it was you : что это мог быть ты
come in : perfective imperative
quite recently : совсем недавно
talking of all sorts of things : разговаривая о всяких вещах
come back : (here) прийти к нам опять
for a few days : на несколько дней

## 22

# AN EXCURSION INTO THE COUNTRY  (I)

Last week we went by train into the country.   At 9.15 we set off for the station which is in the centre of the town.   At the station Father got the tickets, and then we all went on to the platform.   In a few minutes the train came in ;  when it stopped we got into a smoking compartment, as Father wanted to smoke his pipe.   The guard waved his green flag, and the train began to move.   At first it went slowly, but gradually it got faster and faster.   Soon we were hurrying past houses, under bridges, through tunnels ;  the train was going so fast that it was impossible to make out the names of the stations.   As soon as we had got really into the country, we saw men and women working in the fields, and in the meadows horses and cows were lying under the trees.   In an hour and a half the train stopped, and we all got out.

*Notes*

   by train : instrumental
   got (tickets) : bought
   in (a few minutes) : че́рез (acc.)
   smoking compartment : отделе́ние для куря́щих
   began to move : пошёл
   hurry : (here) проноси́ться
   make out : рассмотре́ть
   name (of station) : назва́ние
   had got really into the country : очути́лиеь в настоя́щей дере́вне
   in (fields and meadows) : на

## 23

# AN EXCURSION INTO THE COUNTRY (II)

From the station we walked (for) 20 minutes, first along the main road, and then by a path across beautiful meadows. In some of the meadows the farmers had begun to cut the hay, and the air was full of the sound of the machines and of the merry song of larks.   In front of my uncle's house there is a large pond on which ducks were swimming;  in winter this pond sometimes freezes over, and the farmers and their families from the neighbourhood skate on it whenever it is possible.

When we arrived my uncle was not at home;  my aunt told us that he had gone out early in order to buy some sheep at the market, but that he would be back at one o'clock.   At half-past twelve my cousins came in from school, and at 1.15 we all sat down to dinner.   After dinner my cousins and I went and played in the fields while Mother and Father sat in the garden and chatted to my uncle and aunt.   We left at 4.45 and were home at 7.

*Notes*

by (a path): по + dative
cut the hay: косить сéно
sound: plural
neighbourhood: plural
would be back: вернётся
came in : use прийти
went and played: пошли играть

## 24

# THE CHILDREN AND THE MONKEY

A few days ago my wife saw a crowd of children who were running along the street, shouting and laughing.  Soon she saw an old man with a monkey on his shoulder ;  he had on a green hat and white trousers, and the monkey had on a little red jacket.

Suddenly the monkey jumped down from the old man's shoulder and began dancing about on the pavement.  This delighted the children, and they laughed still more loudly.  But soon the monkey grew tired ;  it jumped up again on to the old man's shoulder and began to lick his face and to kiss him.  The old man patted the monkey, and it was very clear that he and the monkey were great friends.

My wife went into a shop close by and bought some nuts which she gave to the old man for his pet.  The old man thanked her politely, and the monkey became excited when it saw them and tried to snatch the bag from its master's hand.  So the old man put it in his pocket, and soon my wife lost sight of him in the crowd.

*Notes*

he had on . . . .: say, on him were . . .
delight : привести́ в восто́рг
still more loudly : всё гро́мче
to pat : приласка́ть
were great friends : instrumental plural
close by : ближа́йший ; say, a close-by shop
snatch from : вы́хватить из

## 25

# THE DOCTOR VISITS A YOUNG PATIENT

The little grey car stops in front of a big house in Lenin Street, and a man gets out of it with a small bag in his hand. He goes into the house and takes the lift up to the 4th floor; here he rings at the door of flat No. 12. The door is soon opened by a lady who immediately says: " Good morning, Doctor; I am very glad you have come so quickly." The doctor takes off his overcoat and goes with the lady into a small bedroom where a little boy is in bed. He is about 8 years old and is lying quite still, and it seems that he is asleep; but when the doctor speaks, he opens his eyes. The doctor feels his pulse and takes his temperature, and then says: " Have you a headache, Feodor? " " Yes," says the child, " and I am very thirsty." " Is that all? " " Yes," replies Feodor, " but I am rather tired and sleepy." "Well," says the doctor, " you must stay in bed for two or three days, and then you can get up again." He tells the mother that she need not worry, as Feodor has only a chill.

*Notes*

use imperfective present throughout
Lenin Street: у́лица Ле́нина
bag: чемода́нчик
in his hand: say, in his hands
takes lift: поднима́ется по ли́фту
at the door: у две́ри
he is about 8 years old: ему́ о́коло восьми́ лет
still: ти́хо
stay (in bed): say, lie
for two or three days: omit ' for '
she need not: ей не на́до

## 26

## A TRIP ABROAD  (I)

In April we decided to spend a few days in Paris; we had not seen Paris for a long time, and the city always looks gay and attractive in the spring.  We left London early in the morning; there were a lot of people in the train, but we had reserved our seats.  In about $1\frac{1}{2}$ hours we had reached the harbour, and soon went on board the steamer.  Fortunately it was a lovely day; the sun was shining brightly, and the sea was quite calm; so we sat on deck, and were sorry when the time came to disembark.

On the quay we saw a great many porters, who were all shouting loudly.  As soon as the steamer stopped, they rushed on board, and one of them, a big red-faced man in a blue blouse and black trousers, seized our luggage and carried it to the Customs Office.  The Customs Official was very nice and did not examine our cases; so we were soon sitting in the French train and looking out of the window at the crowd of people hurrying to find their seats.

*Notes*

 had not seen : use видáть
 for a long time : давнó
 looks (gay) : вы́глядит + instrumental
 in the spring : instrumental
 there were a lot of people : бы́ло мнóго нарóду
 reserve (seats) : закáзывать, заказáть зарáнее
 in about $1\frac{1}{2}$ hours : приблизи́тельно че́рез полторá часá
 reach : доéхать до
 we were sorry : нам бы́ло досáдно
 to disembark : сходи́ть с парохóда
 **rush** : брóситься

## 27

# A  TRIP  ABROAD  (II)

Half an hour later the train started.   We were surprised to
see that the train actually went along some of the streets
of the old port !   Soon we saw the flat countryside of Northern
France with its long straight roads and rows of poplars and
other trees.   We passed through tiny villages and picturesque
old towns;  old women were sitting in the sun, making lace
or knitting, and chatting in front of their cottages.   In one
village we saw a little girl driving a cow along the road, and
in another a man was leading some goats and playing a pipe.

Between the port and the capital the train stopped once, and
we took advantage of the stop in order to get out and buy some
French newspapers and drink a cup of real French coffee in
the station restaurant.   As we left the station again, we could
see the old cathedral with its beautiful Gothic towers and
lovely windows.   Shortly after this darkness fell, and it was
quite dark when we reached Paris.

*Notes*

  the train started : поезд пошёл
  we were surprised to see : мы видели с удивлением, как
  passed : проехали мимо (+ gen.)
  make lace : плести кружево
  drive (a cow) : гнать
  station restaurant : ресторан на станции
  leave (station) : выехать с (+ gen.)
  we could see : say, we saw (perf.)

## 28

# ALLIES WANT TO UNDERSTAND EACH OTHER

During the war, England and the Soviet Union became allies, and both countries want to understand each other better.  Many English people have begun to learn Russian, and they are glad when they can read a Russian newspaper or a Russian author in the original language.  A great many people too are interested in Russia, although they are not studying the language.  In the U.S.S.R., too, people are very much interested in England, and want to know all they can about England and English life.

Many of the young people of both countries have begun to correspond with each other, generally in their native language.  When a letter from Russia arrives in England, it is translated into English and then sent to the address of a correspondent, and vice versa.  In this way the young people can learn what their friends in a foreign country are doing in schools, in factories, on the farms and in the towns.

*Notes*

> have become allies: instrumental plural
> in the original language: в оригинáле
> many of the young people: мнóгие из молодёжи
> it is translated . . . and sent: перевóдят егó . . . и посылáют егó
> to the address: по áдресу
> learn (in last sentence): узнáть

## 29

# A LETTER FROM THE U.S.S.R.

Dear English friend,

I send you hearty greetings from the U.S.S.R. I was very glad when your letter came, and I am writing to you at once. I hope you will receive my answer, and that we shall write many letters to each other.

Now I will tell you a little about myself : I am 16 years old, and I go to school in the town of M. My father is a Red Army man, and I have not seen him for a long time ; I have no brothers or sisters, and I live here with my mother in the middle of a thick forest. Not far from our house there is a river in which there are a lot of fish. In the summer I often spend the whole day by the river. Of course in the winter the river freezes over, and then we go skating on it, and travel on sledges through the forest, or else we go skiing. I do not think that you ski in England, but I think it is sometimes cold enough to skate, for I have seen pictures of skaters on ponds in the London parks.

Last winter we clearly heard the noise of the guns, as our troops were fighting only about 20 kilometres away. We were afraid that we should have to leave our home, but fortunately our army drove the Hitler troops back.

Your Russian friend,

MICHAEL

*Notes*

you : 2nd singular
have not seen : видáть
I am 16 years old : say, to me 16 years
through the forest : пó лесу
cold enough to . . . : достáточно хóлодно, чтóбы . . .
pictures : картúнки
about 20 km. away : киломéтрах в двадцатú
should have to : future
drive back : отогнáть

## 30

## CHEKHOV

Recently a friend and I went to the theatre to see Chekhov's *Uncle Vanya*.   This was the first time we had seen one of his plays, and we found the performance very interesting.   The characters are natural, they are ordinary people, but like most of the people in Chekhov's plays, they lead an aimless life.   They themselves are unhappy, and yet do not seem able to alter this.   In the play there are comic episodes, but the comic element is often much nearer to tragedy, as often happens in life.

Chekhov is well-known both in his country and abroad as a writer of plays and short stories.   His plays were first produced at the Moscow Art Theatre, and they are fairly often produced in London.   Besides *Uncle Vanya*, performances are given of *The Seagull*, *Three Sisters* and *The Cherry Orchard*. Chekhov's widow, who now (1947) is an old lady, acted in all her husband's plays at the Art Theatre, and she said recently that her favourite part is that of Lyubov Ranevskaya in *The Cherry Orchard*.

*Notes*

    (found) very interesting : instrumental
    do not seem able : say, it seems that they are not able
    much nearer to tragedy : гораздо ближе к трагедии
    were produced : были поставлены
    performances are given of : даются
    that of : omit

## 31

# WHAT WE SAW FROM THE TRAIN

It was a beautiful day, and as we travelled north we were very much surprised to see so few villages.  We saw very few houses and very few people in the fields.  From time to time we caught sight of some wooden houses, but as we did not pass through any large towns and only very few villages, the country seemed to us very empty.  Even the villages ended with the stations; as soon as the train had left the platform, we were in the middle of fields or forests again.  I think that the forests and lakes must produce a deep impression upon a foreigner who travels there, especially upon an Englishman. The forests of pine and birch are very dense and very different from our English woods, and the lakes, both large and small, are almost innumerable.  Everywhere the people are very friendly and ready to help a foreigner, even if he cannot understand their language.

## 32

# WE VISIT OUR FRIENDS

We had walked for two hours, but had not yet found the house we were looking for.  At last we saw it; it stood not far from the road, behind tall trees.  We went up to the front door and rang the bell.  When we went in, we took off our hats and left them and our coats in the hall; then we went into the room where our friends were sitting.  As we had breakfasted early, we were very hungry, and soon we sat down to table  After a very delicious lunch we went out into the garden and chatted for a couple of hours with our friends; the ladies smoked cigarettes, but the men preferred their pipes. The weather was fine, the sun was shining brightly, and the birds were singing in the trees.  When our friends bought this house three years ago, there was nothing in the garden, but they have worked a great deal in it, and now it is really beautiful.   Not far from the house is a small lake where they often bathe and swim.   They invited us to visit them again soon, and we hope to go there next week

## 83

## LIFE IN LONDON 50 YEARS AGO (I)

I was born in London in 1895 and have spent nearly all my life there.   The suburb in which my parents lived was very pleasant, and there were several parks there where my brother and I used to go nearly every day when we were children; we used to play various games in the park and we often fed the ducks on the pond.

In my childhood the omnibuses and trams were drawn by horses, and there were no taxis, but horse-cabs.   The streets were not as clean as now-a-days, but old men, women, and even children used to sweep them where people crossed frequently.   The Underground had been fairly recently built; some of its trains even had steam-engines, and the smoke from them used to come up through holes in the streets.

People then dressed very differently; the ladies' skirts were so long that they touched the ground, the men wore top-hats, frock-coats and kid gloves, and always took a stick or an umbrella with them.   It is interesting and amusing to look at pictures which represent life in London at the end of the 19th century and the beginning of the 20th.

## 34

# LIFE IN LONDON 50 YEARS AGO  (II)

I left school when I was 17 and began work in the office of a friend of my father's who was a lawyer.  The office was rather a long way from our house, and I had to go by omnibus each day and had to leave home at 8.15 in order to arrive there at 9.0.  The top of the buses was open, and the driver sat on a high box in front of the passengers; I used to like to sit by him and talk to him as we went along the streets.  When it rained, the passengers used to open their umbrellas in order to protect themselves.

Sometimes when we woke up in the morning, we saw that there was a thick fog; I had to go to the office all the same, but of course I arrived rather late.  Foreigners often say that England and especially London, is always covered by fog during the winter months; this is an exaggeration which amuses Londoners, who know that even in winter the weather is often fine and clear.  It is true that sometimes even now-a-days the fog is rather thick, but it does not last long, and it is not so yellow or dirty as it was at the beginning of the century.

## 35

# MODERN SCIENCE

If we compare the world now-a-days with the world as it was 100 years ago, the difference is amazing.  In nearly all branches of human activity science has enabled us to make great changes in our manner of life.  We see and use very many things now-a-days which our ancestors never dreamed of, for example the telephone, the telegraph, the motor-car, the radio and the aeroplane. A century ago there were not many railways, and people had to go by stage-coach or on horseback, and steamers had not completely replaced sailing-ships. A voyage from England to America often lasted weeks or months, but now-a-days an aeroplane can fly across the Atlantic in a few hours. Medical knowledge has also increased very much, and surgeons are able to perform wonderful operations and to save the lives of sick people who would certainly have died 100 years ago. But modern science has also helped men to invent things which have brought a great deal of suffering to mankind, e.g. bombs and torpedoes. So when people talk of the great achievements of modern science, we must not forget these horrible things.

# RUSSIAN PASSAGES

## КОТЁНОК

Бы́ли брат и сестра́—Ва́ся и Ка́тя, и у них была́ ко́шка. Весно́й ко́шка пропа́ла. Де́ти иска́ли её везде́, но не могли́ найти́. Оди́н раз они́ игра́ли по́дле амба́ра и услы́шали— над голово́й что́-то мяу́чит то́нкими голоса́ми. Ва́ся влез по ле́стнице под кры́шу амба́ра. А Ка́тя стоя́ла внизу́ и всё спра́шивала : ,, Нашёл ? Нашёл ?‘‘ Но Ва́ся не отвеча́л ей. Наконе́ц Ва́ся закрича́л ей : ,, Нашёл ! На́ша ко́шка . . . и у ней котя́та,—каки́е чуде́сные ; иди́ сюда́ скоре́е.‘‘

Ка́тя побежа́ла домо́й, доста́ла молока́ и принесла́ ко́шке. Котя́т бы́ло пять. Когда́ они́ вы́росли немно́жко и ста́ли вылеза́ть из-под угла́, де́ти вы́брали себе́ одного́ котёнка, се́рого с бе́лыми ла́пками, и принесли́ в дом. Мать раздала́ всех остальны́х котя́т, а э́того оста́вила де́тям.

Де́ти корми́ли его́, игра́ли с ним и кла́ли с собо́й спать.

Оди́н раз де́ти пошли́ игра́ть на доро́гу и взя́ли с собо́й котёнка.

Вдруг они́ услы́шали, что кто́-то гро́мко кричи́т : ,, Наза́д, наза́д !‘‘ и увида́ли, что ска́чет охо́тник, а впереди́ него́ две соба́ки увида́ли котёнка и хотя́т схвати́ть его́. А котёнок, глу́пый, вме́сто того́ чтобы бежа́ть, присе́л к земле́, сго́рбил спи́ну и смо́трит на соба́к. Ка́тя испуга́лась соба́к, закрича́ла и побежа́ла прочь от них. А Ва́ся <u>что́ было ду́ху</u> [1] пусти́лся к котёнку и в одно́ вре́мя с соба́ками под- бежа́л к нему́. Соба́ки хоте́ли схвати́ть котёнка, но Ва́ся упа́л живото́м на котёнка и закры́л его́ от соба́к.

[1] As fast as he could.

Охотник подскакал и отогнал собак, а Вася принёс домой котёнка и уже больше не брал его с собой в поле.

## ВОПРОСЫ

1. Как зовут этих детей?
2. Какое животное было у них?
3. Что случилось однажды весной?
4. Где дети играли?
5. Что они услыхали?
6. Как Вася влез под крышу амбара?
7. Что он нашёл там?
8. Зачем Катя побежала домой?
9. Сколько было котят?
10. Какого котёнка дети выбрали себе?
11. Что мать сделала с остальными котятами?
12. Кого дети увидали один раз на дороге?
13. Что собаки хотели сделать, когда увидали котёнка?
14. Что сделал котёнок?
15. Как Вася спас котёнка от собак?

# В СТА́РОЙ МОСКВЕ́

## Глава́ 1-ая

Это бы́ло давно́, мы жи́ли в Москве́ в ма́леньком деревя́нном до́ме, каки́х бо́льше уже́ нет, на ти́хой боково́й у́лице; э́ти у́лицы называ́ются в Росси́и переу́лками.

В на́шем до́ме бы́ло два этажа́, внизу́ жи́ли мы, хозя́ева до́ма, а наверху́ бы́ли две кварти́ры поме́ньше, в кото́рых жи́ли квартира́нты. Дом был ста́рый, постро́енный в нача́ле 19-го столе́тия. Деревя́нные воро́та с кали́ткой отделя́ли двор от у́лицы, и подъе́зд к до́му был со двора́. На дворе́ бы́ли слу́жбы: сара́й для экипа́жей, коню́шня, по́греб, в кото́ром храни́лись запа́сы овоще́й и други́х проду́ктов; в конце́ зимы́ по́греб набива́лся льдом,[1] кото́рый сохраня́лся до о́сени. Как прия́тно бы́ло в жа́ркий ле́тний день вы́пить холо́дного ква́су со льда́! Придёшь, быва́ло, в по́греб[2] в тако́й день, откро́ют тебе́ люк, закрыва́ющий глубо́кую я́му напо́лненную льдом, и пахнёт на тебя́ отту́да хо́лодом и све́жестью!

За дворо́м был большо́й сад с фрукто́выми дере́вьями, куста́ми мали́ны и сморо́дины. В конце́ са́да была́ бесе́дка. В э́той бесе́дке весно́й и́ли ле́том, когда́ быва́ло жа́рко и ду́шно в ко́мнатах, мы пи́ли чай и иногда́ в ти́хие ле́тние вечера́ у́жинали. Пе́ред бесе́дкой была́ больша́я клу́мба с цвета́ми, в середи́не кото́рой рос большо́й куст шипо́вника, а у вхо́да в бесе́дку росли́ кусты́ сире́ни и жасми́на; как они́ па́хли весно́й, како́й арома́т наполня́л сад!

Да́же тепе́рь, как заслы́шу за́пах сире́ни или жасми́на, то́тчас же пе́редо мной встаю́т карти́ны счастли́вого де́тства —наш сад, на́ши весёлые ле́тние дни и вечера́, проведённые в нём. Круго́м нас бы́ли таки́е же сады́, в одно́м из них был

---

[1] In the cellar a deep pit used to be dug and covered by a trap-door (люк); towards the end of the winter this pit was filled with ice so as to help to keep food good during the hot weather.

[2] The word бывало, coupled with the future perfective, gives the idea of habit, recurrence; translate by some such phrase as: "You would come into the cellar."

даже пруд; э́тот сад был бо́льше на́шего и каза́лся нам
таи́нственным, необыкнове́нным, потому́ что там никого́
никогда́ не́ было.

## ВОПРО́СЫ

### Глава́ 1-ая

1. Где мы жи́ли? в како́м го́роде?
2. Как называ́ются боковы́е у́лицы?
3. Что отделя́ло двор от у́лицы?
4. Ско́лько бы́ло этаже́й в на́шем до́ме?
5. Где жи́ли мы?
6. Кто жил наверху́?
7. Каки́е постро́йки бы́ли на дворе́?
8. Что храни́лось в по́гребе?
9. Почему́ бы́ло прия́тно входи́ть в по́греб в жа́ркий
   ле́тний день?
10. Каки́е бы́ли дере́вья в саду́, цветы́?
11. Где росли́ цветы́?
12. Что мы де́лали в бесе́дке?
13. Почему́ сосе́дний сад каза́лся нам таи́нственным?

### Глава́ 2-ая

В на́шей кварти́ре бы́ло семь ко́мнат. При вхо́де в дом
была́ ма́ленькая пере́дняя, кото́рая называ́лась се́ни,[1] а за
ней друга́я, побо́льше. Нале́во из пере́дней была́ за́ла, а
ря́дом с за́лой—гости́ная. О́кна в за́ле выходи́ли на две
сто́роны [2]—на у́лицу и во двор. С у́лицы о́кна на́ ночь
закрыва́лись деревя́нными ста́внями.

В за́ле в одно́м углу́ стоя́л роя́ль, а вдоль стен два ка́рточ-
ных стола́ и сту́лья. На стена́х висе́ли две ла́мпы, кото́рые
освеща́ли ко́мнату мя́гким, прия́тным све́том. На о́кнах
висе́ли бе́лые што́ры, кото́рые поднима́лись и опуска́лись.

---

[1] This is a small entrance-hall or corridor between the front door and
inner door, and helps to keep the cold from the interior of the house.

[2] The windows looked out on two sides.

Пол в за́ле был парке́тный, всегда́ блестя́щий, хорошо́ отполиро́ванный ; на э́том полу́ бы́ло о́чень хорошо́ танцова́ть, а танцова́ть мы о́чень люби́ли.

С гости́ной за́ла соединя́лась а́ркой, и о́бе ко́мнаты бы́ли как бы продолже́нием одна́ друго́й.[1] В гости́ной стоя́ла мя́гкая ме́бель, оби́тая што́фом ; пе́ред дива́ном был ова́льный стол с большо́й краси́вой ла́мпой посреди́не, а круго́м стоя́ли четы́ре кре́сла. У противополо́жной стены́ был стекля́нный шкаф с фарфо́ром и серебро́м и со стари́нными хруста́льными ва́зами. На о́кнах висе́ли кисе́йные занаве́ски, а на полу́ лежа́л то́лстый, пуши́стый ковёр.

Э́ти ко́мнаты употребля́лись бо́льшею ча́стью, когда́ у нас быва́ли го́сти ; обы́чная же жизнь проходи́ла во вну́тренних ко́мнатах—в спа́льнях и столо́вой.

В спа́льнях не то́лько спа́ли, но проводи́ли бо́льшую часть вре́мени : в них рабо́тали, учи́лись, болта́ли, игра́ли. В спа́льнях кро́ме крова́тей и комо́дов была́ и друга́я ме́бель : столы́, по́лки с кни́гами, кре́сла, что де́лало ко́мнату ую́тной.

Для отопле́ния до́ма бы́ли пе́чи, высо́кие до потолка́, сде́ланные из кирпиче́й покры́тых снару́жи гля́нцем ; э́ти пе́чи топи́лись дрова́ми раз в су́тки, они́ о́чень хорошо́ держа́ли тепло́, и тепло́ э́то бы́ло сухо́е и прия́тное.

За спа́льнями была́ столо́вая и буфе́тная, а за ни́ми ку́хня с большо́й ру́сской пе́чью.

[1] **Were a kind of continuation one of the other.** как бы = as if.


# ВОПРО́СЫ

### Глава́ 2-а́я

1. Ско́лько ко́мнат бы́ло в на́шей кварти́ре?
2. Куда́ выходи́ли о́кна в за́ле?
3. Что стоя́ло в углу́ в за́ле?
4. Что висе́ло на стена́х?
5. Како́й пол был в за́ле?

6. Что мы люби́ли де́лать в за́ле?
7. Кака́я ме́бель стоя́ла в гости́ной?
8. Что храни́лось в стекля́нном шкафу́?
9. Что лежа́ло на полу́ в гости́ной?
10. Для кого́ предназнача́лись э́ти ко́мнаты?
11. Где проходи́ла обы́чная жизнь?
12. Что де́лали в спа́льнях?
13. Кака́я ме́бель находи́лась там?
14. Как ота́пливался наш дом?

## Глава́ 3-тья

Жизнь в до́ме начина́лась ра́но, часо́в в семь, когда́ встава́л оте́ц, за ним встава́ла мать и мы. К восьми́ часа́м в столо́вой уже́ кипе́л самова́р, стол был накры́т, мы бы́стро выпива́ли чай, съеда́ли на́-спех бу́лки или хлеб с ма́слом и уходи́ли, кто на слу́жбу, кто в шко́лу, в университе́т, смотря́ по во́зрасту.

К четырём часа́м мы все возвраща́лись домо́й, обе́дали, оте́ц и мать шли отдыха́ть, де́ти сади́лись за уро́ки, а взро́слые и́ли рабо́тали, чита́ли, уходи́ли в теа́тр, в го́сти, и́ли кто-нибу́дь приходи́л к нам. В де́сять часо́в у́жинали и шли спать. Так проходи́ла и́зо дня в день на́ша жизнь с её ма́ленькими и больши́ми ра́достями и огорче́ниями; её однообра́зие наруша́ли пра́здники и ле́тние кани́кулы, когда́ все бы́ли до́ма. Тогда́ дом наполня́лся гостя́ми, молодёжью, шу́мом, весе́льем. По вечера́м устра́ивались та́нцы, и́гры, ста́вились да́же спекта́кли, устра́ивались пое́здки за́ город.

Конча́лись пра́здники и сно́ва начина́лась та́-же бу́дничная жизнь.

Ле́том мы обыкнове́нно уезжа́ли на да́чу, куда́-нибу́дь недалеко́ от Москвы́, в дере́вню. Остава́ться в го́роде бы́ло о́чень неприя́тно, пы́льно и ду́шно. Вся́кий, кто мог, стара́лся уе́хать из го́рода. Три ле́тних ме́сяца в центра́льной Росси́и о́чень жа́ркие и сухи́е. А в дере́вне была́ благода́ть—просто́р поле́й, тени́стые леса́, река́ и́ли ре́чка, и́ли пруд, где мо́жно бы́ло купа́ться, уди́ть ры́бу, ката́ться на ло́дке. Ско́лько удово́льствий, како́е наслажде́ние чу́вствовать себя́ на свобо́де, вне ка́менной городско́й духоты́. Ле́тние кани́кулы продолжа́лись в шко́лах и вы́сших уче́бных заведе́ниях с ию́ня до полови́ны а́вгуста и́ли нача́ла сентября́. Те, кто служи́л, е́здили ка́ждое у́тро в го́род и возвраща́лись к ве́черу на да́чу. На желе́зных доро́гах бы́ли да́же специа́льные да́чные поезда́.

## ВОПРО́СЫ

### Глава́ 3-тья

1. Когда́ начина́лась жизнь в до́ме?
2. Кто встава́л пе́рвым?
3. Когда́ встава́ли мы?
4. Что мы пи́ли и е́ли за у́тренним за́втраком?
5. В кото́ром часу́ мы возвраща́лись?
6. Как мы проводи́ли вре́мя по́сле обе́да?
7. Чем конча́лся наш день?
8. Как мы проводи́ли пра́здники?
9. Где мы проводи́ли ле́то?
10. Почему́ мы уезжа́ли на да́чу?
11. Каки́е бы́ли развлече́ния на да́че?
12. Ско́лько и каки́е ме́сяцы продолжа́лись кани́кулы?

---

1. Опиши́те дом, где вы провели́ ва́ше де́тство.
2. Как вы проводи́ли вре́мя, когда́ вы бы́ли детьми́, взро́слыми?

# ДЕНЬ В СЕМЬЕ

Муж—Ива́н Петро́вич Васи́льев.
Жена́—А́нна Серге́евна Васи́льева.
Ма́ша—дома́шняя помо́щница
А́ня—ста́ршая дочь, 12 лет
Ва́ня—сын—10 лет.
Ле́на—мла́дшая дочь, 8 лет.

## Де́йствие 1-ое

*А́нна Серге́евна:* Ма́ша, накро́йте на стол, пора́ обе́дать, Ива́н Петро́вич ско́ро придёт со слу́жбы,[1] да и де́ти сейча́с верну́тся из шко́лы.

*Ма́ша:* Сейча́с! Каки́е таре́лки поста́вить? Каки́е положи́ть ножи́ и ви́лки? Что вы бу́дете ку́шать?

*А С.:* Пе́рвое блю́до—ры́ба, поэ́тому положи́те ры́бные ножи́, а сла́дкое—пу́динг. Не забу́дьте поста́вить графи́н и стака́ны для воды́, а для Ива́на Петро́вича рю́мку, он лю́бит вы́пить рю́мочку во́дки пе́ред обе́дом.

*Ма́ша:* Принесла́ ли пра́чка салфе́тки? мне ка́жется, что э́ти не доста́точно чи́стые, и их на́до перемени́ть.

*А. С.:* Да, чи́стые в сре́днем я́щике буфе́та, а гря́зные положи́те в ни́жний, я отошлю́ их к пра́чке. Ах, вот и де́ти! Здра́вствуйте, мои́ ми́ленькие! На дворе́ ве́рно о́чень хо́лодно?

*Де́ти:* Да, ма́мочка, ужа́сно хо́лодно, мы совсе́м замёрзли.

*А. С.:* Раздева́йтесь. Снима́йте скоре́е шу́бы и бо́тики. Де́вочки, иди́те в де́тскую, переоде́ньтесь во что-нибу́дь потепле́е. А ты, Ва́ня, перемени́ то́лько башмаки́, у тебя́ то́лстый костю́м, в нём не озя́бнешь. Поспеши́те, па́па сейча́с придёт.

*А́ня:* Ма́мочка, мо́жно мне наде́ть голубу́ю вя́заную ко́фточку и си́нюю ю́бку? Я их о́чень люблю́.

---

[1] From the office.

*А. С.:* Хорошо, надень, если тебе хочется, а ты, Лена, надень красненькое фланелевое платьице, оно очень нравится папе, помнишь, как он сказал: ,, оно очень идёт моей маленькой дочурке, она в нём совсём взрослая.‘‘

(Дети уходят)

## ВОПРОСЫ

### Действие 1-ое

1. Как зовут детей Васильевых?
2. Сколько им лет?
3. Откуда приходит отец?
4. Откуда приходят дети?
5. Что они будут кушать сегодня?
6. Что Маша должна поставить для Ивана Петровича?
7. Почему ему нужна рюмка?
8. Какая была погода?
9. Что дети должны сделать в детской?
10. Какое платье Аня хочет надеть?
11. Почему платье Лены нравится её отцу?

### Действие 2-ое

*Иван Петрович:* Здравствуй, Аня, как ты?  Здорова?

*А. С.:* Ничего себе,[1] только очень устала.  А как ты?

*И. П.:* Сегодня у меня в больнице был очень тяжёлый день—доктор Павлов в отпуску, я должен был осмотреть не только своих, но и его пациентов, а их было около пятидесяти человек.

*А. С.:* Ах ты, мой бедный Ваничка; ну ничего, у нас сегодня твой любимый обед, рыба под белым соусом. Пообедаешь, посидишь—отдохнёшь, я расскажу тебе, что я делала сегодня, послушаем радио, и ты опять почувствуешь себя бодрым и весёлым.

---

[1] **So-so, not too bad.**

*И. П.:* Да, конéчно, мúлая ты моя́ жёнушка! Где дéти? Пришлú из шкóлы?

*А. С.:* Да, онú пошлú переодевáться.

*И. П.:* Отлúчно, пойдý помы́ться—бýду сейчáс готóв.

*А. С.:* Идú, а я скажý подавáть на стол.[1] Дéти, готóвы? Пáпа пришёл, идúте сюдá скорéе.

*Дéти:* Вот и мы, мáмочка.

*А. С.:* Ся́дем здесь, поболтáем покá пáпа сойдёт. Расскажúте мне, чтó бы́ло в шкóле, мнóго ли вам зáдали урóков?

*Вáня:* У меня́ немнóго, у нас нé было францýзского, учúтель заболéл, и я сдéлал половúну урóков в шкóле. Знáешь, учúтель механúки объясня́л нам сегóдня констрýкцию самолёта, ужáсно интерéсно, я непремéнно бýду лётчиком.

*Áня:* А у меня́ довóльно мнóго. Меня́ сегóдня спрáшивали по истóрии, я óчень хорошó отвечáла, и учúтельница остáлась мной óчень довóльна.[2]

*А. С.:* А ты, моя́ мáленькая птúчка, почемý молчúшь, ты здорóва? Подú ко мне, мой голýбчик, дай мне попрóбовать твою́ голóвку, нет ли у тебя́ жáру? не болúт ли онá?

*Лéна:* Нет, мáмочка, немнóго устáла, вот и всё.

*А. С.:* А вот и пáпа.

*И. П.:* Здрáвствуйте, дéти, как вы? здорóвы, в шкóле всё в поря́дке?

*Дéти:* Здрáвствуй, пáпочка, всё отлúчно!

*И. П.:* Ну, éсли так, давáйте садúться за стол, я гóлоден как волк, дýмаю, что и вы тóже. А . . а сегóдня щи! в такóй морóзный день óчень хорошó съесть тарéлку горя́чих щей. А почемý нет пирожкóв?

*А. С.:* Не успéла сдéлать, пóздно вернýлась из гóрода. Ты свобóден сегóдня вéчером?

---

[1] To serve the meal.
[2] Was pleased with me.

*И. П.:*  Да, заседа́ние на́шего комите́та слу́жащих отло́-
жено на за́втра, а парти́йное собра́ние до четверга́,
сейча́с-же по́сле слу́жбы; я не приду́ домо́й обе́дать,
съем что-нибу́дь в на́шей служе́бной столо́вой, оста́вь
мне что-нибу́дь поу́жинать.

*А. С.:*  Э́то зна́чит, что мы мо́жем провести́ ны́нешний ве́чер
все вме́сте; я свобо́дна, О́льга Ива́новна дежу́рит в
домо́вом комите́те, де́ти ра́но ко́нчат уро́ки и посидя́т
с на́ми, вы́пьем ча́ю, послу́шаем ра́дио, сего́дня
ве́чером о́чень хоро́шая програ́мма; проведём ве́чер
по семе́йному,[1] что́ нам не всегда́ удаётся.

---

[1] all together (lit.: in family fashion)

# ВОПРО́СЫ

## Де́йствие 2-о́е

1. Как Ива́н Петро́вич провёл день?
2. Ско́лько бы́ло у него́ пацие́нтов?
3. Что А́нна Серге́евна собира́ется рассказа́ть по́сле обе́да?
4. Что Ива́н Петро́вич де́лает пе́ред обе́дом?
5. Почему́ у Ва́ни не́ было францу́зского уро́ка?
6. Почему́ ему́ интере́сно объясне́ние констру́кции само-лёта?
7. На како́м уро́ке А́ня отве́тила о́чень хорошо́?
8. Как мы зна́ем, что Ива́н Петро́вич го́лоден?
9. Како́й у них суп сего́дня?
10. Когда́ бу́дет у Ива́на Петро́вича заседа́ние комите́та?
11. Где он бу́дет обе́дать в четве́рг?
12. Как семья́ собира́лась провести́ ве́чер?

D

### Действие 3-тье

*А. С.:* Ну, вот тепе́рь ты мо́жешь отдохну́ть, сади́сь в своё
любѝмое кре́сло, а я расскажу́ тебе́, что́ со мной
случѝлось сего́дня у́тром.

*И. П.:* Дай то́лько закури́ть, хо́чешь папиро́су?

*А. С.:* Нет, я уже́ вы́курила сего́дня две. Подожди́ не-
мно́го, я принесу́ мою́ рабо́чую коро́бку, мне на́до
ко́е-что починѝть.

*И. П.:* Сади́сь вот сюда́, на дива́н у стола́, вот тебе́ ла́мпа;
тепе́рь расска́зывай.

*А. С.:* Ты зна́ешь, что мне бы́ло ну́жно купи́ть не́сколько
веще́й для тебя́ и для дете́й. По́сле у́треннего за́втрака
я вы́шла, се́ла на углу́ в авто́бус, заплати́ла за биле́т
ме́лочью, кото́рая была́ у меня́ в карма́не и дое́хала до
у́лицы Го́рького, где я сошла́ с авто́буса. В уни-
верса́льном магази́не я купи́ла, что́ мне бы́ло ну́жно:
не́сколько пар чуло́к и носко́в, три блу́зки, две для
де́вочек и одну́ для себя́, шесть воротнико́в для твои́х
ста́рых руба́шек и о́чень краси́вый га́лстук, кото́рый
тебе́ наве́рно понра́вится. Посмотре́ла пальто́ для
себя́, мне хо́чется купи́ть что-нибу́дь к весне́, моё
ста́рое уж о́чень пло́хо, но к сожале́нию не нашла́
ничего́ подходя́щего. Наконе́ц я ко́нчила все поку́пки
и должна́ была́ заплати́ть за них. Открыва́ю су́мку, а
кошелька́-то в ней и нет.[1] Смотрю́, ищу́—нигде́ нет!
Не могу́ поня́ть, что́ случѝлось. По доро́ге я не
открыва́ла су́мки, ты по́мнишь, я тебе́ сказа́ла, что я
заплати́ла за биле́т ме́лочью, кото́рая была́ в карма́не
пальто́. Су́мку держа́ла всё вре́мя в рука́х. Никто́
не мог откры́ть её и вы́нуть кошелёк. Очеви́дно я
оста́вила де́ньги до́ма. Я ужа́сно испуга́лась, что́
тепе́рь де́лать, ка́к сказа́ть прика́зчику, что у меня́ нет
де́нег, что́бы заплати́ть за ку́пленные ве́щи? Я была́
в отча́янии, покрасне́ла и чуть не распла́калась.
Вдруг поднима́ю глаза́ и кого́-же ви́жу? как ты
ду́маешь?

[1] **My purse just wasn't there.**

*И. П.:* Трудно угадать, кто был твой ангел-спаситель.

*А. С.:* Тётя Саша!—стоит передо мной и с удивлением смотрит, почему я красная и взволнованная. Ты знаешь, я очень люблю тётю Сашу и всегда очень рада её видеть, но никогда в жизни я не радовалась ей так, как обрадовалась тут. Я объяснила ей, что случилось и в каком я была затруднении. К счастью она только что была в банке, где взяла деньги ; у неё оказалось достаточно, чтобы заплатить за свои и мои покупки. Мы расплатились и пошли завтракать в ресторан. За завтраком я ещё раз рассказала ей мою историю, мы посмеялись и я успокоилась.

*И. П.:* Какая ты рассеянная ; ну как можно выходить из дому, не посмотрев, всё ли ты взяла !

*А. С.:* Не брани меня, я сама знаю, что я очень часто забываю вещи, но право-же, это может случиться со всяким.

## ВОПРОСЫ

### Действие 3-тье

1. Куда Иван Петрович садится ?
2. Что ему расскажет его жена ?
3. Почему она не хочет папиросы ?
4. Чем она заплатила за билет в автобусе ?
5. Что она сделала, когда автобус доехал до улицы Горького ?
6. В какой магазин она вошла ?
7. Что она купила там ?
8. Что она нашла, когда она открыла свою сумку ?
9. Как она чувствовала себя, узнав что у неё нет денег ?
10. Кем была для неё тётя Саша ?
11. Где была тётя Саша, прежде чем она пришла в магазин ?
12. Почему она могла заплатить за все покупки ?
13. Куда обе дамы пошли после этого, и почему ?
14. Что Иван Петрович сказал своей жене, услышав эту историю ?
15. Что ответила ему Анна Сергеевна ?

## ЛЕ́БЕДИ

Ле́беди ста́дом лете́ли из холо́дной страны́ в тёплые зе́мли. Они́ лете́ли че́рез мо́ре. Они́ лете́ли день и ночь, и друго́й день и другу́ю ночь они́ не отдыха́я лете́ли над водо́ю. На не́бе был по́лный ме́сяц, и ле́беди далеко́ внизу́ под собо́ю ви́дели сине́ющую во́ду. Все ле́беди уста́ли, маха́я кры́льями, но не остана́вливались и лете́ли да́льше. Впереди́ лете́ли ста́рые, си́льные ле́беди, сза́ди лете́ли те, кото́рые бы́ли моло́же и слабе́е. Оди́н молодо́й ле́бедь лете́л позади́ всех. Си́лы его́ ослабе́ли. Наконе́ц он не мог лете́ть да́льше. Тогда́ он, распусти́в кры́лья, пошёл кни́зу. Он бли́же и бли́же спуска́лся к воде́, а това́рищи его́ да́льше и да́льше беле́лись в ме́сячном све́те. Ле́бедь опусти́лся на́ воду и сложи́л кры́лья.

Ста́до лебеде́й чуть видне́лось бе́лой чертой́[1] на све́тлом не́бе. И чуть слы́шно бы́ло в тишине́, как звене́ли их кры́лья. Когда́ они́ совсе́м скры́лись из ви́да, ле́бедь заки́нул наза́д ше́ю и закры́л глаза́. Он не шевели́лся, и то́лько мо́ре поднима́ло и опуска́ло его́. Пе́ред заре́й лёгкий ветеро́к стал колыха́ть мо́ре. И вода́ плеска́ла в бе́лую грудь ле́бедя. Ле́бедь откры́л глаза́. На восто́ке красне́ла заря́, и ме́сяц и звёзды ста́ли бледне́е. Ле́бедь вздохну́л, вы́тянул ше́ю и, взмахну́в кры́льями, приподня́лся и полете́л, цепля́я кры́льями по воде́. Он поднима́лся вы́ше и вы́ше, и когда́ вода́ оста́лась далеко́ внизу́ его́, он полете́л вперёд, в ту сто́рону, где бы́ли тёплые стра́ны. Он лете́л оди́н над та́йными во́дами туда́, куда́ улете́ли его́ това́рищи.

---

[1] Like a white streak (instrumental of comparison).

## ВОПРО́СЫ

1. Куда́ лете́ли ле́беди?
2. Как до́лго они́ лете́ли?
3. Как они́ лете́ли?

4. Кто летéл позадú всех?
5. Почемý он не мог летéть дáльше?
6. Кудá он опустúлся?
7. Что он сдéлал, когдá опустúлся нá воду?
8. Что разбудúло лéбедя?
9. Что сдéлал лéбедь, когдá он проснýлся?
10. Кудá он полетéл?

---

Сравнúте лéбедя с лётчиком.

## ПРЫЖÓК

Одúн корáбль обошёл вокрýг свéта и возвращáлся домóй. Былá тúхая погóда, весь нарóд был на пáлубе. Посредú нарóда вертéлась большáя обезьяна и забавляла всех. Обезьяна эта кóрчилась, прыгала, дéлала смешнýе рóжи, передрáзнивала людéй, и вúдно бýло—онá знáла, что éю забавляются.

Онá прыгнула к двенадцатилéтнему мáльчику, сýну капитáна корабля, сорвалá с егó головý шляпу, надéла и жúво взобралáсь на мáчту. Все засмеялись, а мáльчик остáлся без шляпы и сам не знал, смеяться ли емý úли сердúться.[1]

Обезьяна сéла на пéрвой переклáдине мáчты, снялá шляпу и стáла зубáми и лáпами рвать её. Онá как бýдто дразнúла мáльчика, покáзывала на негó и дéлала емý рóжи.

Мáльчик крúкнул на неё. Матрóсы грóмче стáли смеяться, а мáльчик покраснéл, скúнул кýртку и брóсился за обезьяной на мáчту. В однý минýту он взобрáлся по верёвке на пéрвую переклáдину, но обезьяна ещё ловчéе и быстрéе егó взобралáсь ещё выше.

—Так не уйдёшь же ты от меня!—закричáл мáльчик и полéз ещё выше.

Обезьяна опять подманúла егó, полéзла ещё выше, но мáльчик не отставáл. Так обезьяна и мáльчик в однý минýту добралúсь до сáмого вéрха.

[1] Whether to laugh or to be angry.

На са́мом верху́ обезья́на вы́тянулась во всю длину́ и, зацепи́вшись за́дней руко́й за верёвку, пове́сила шля́пу на край после́дней перекла́дины, а сама́ взобрала́сь на маку́шку ма́чты и отту́да пока́зывала зу́бы и ра́довалась.

От ма́чты до конца́ перекла́дины, где висе́ла шля́па, бы́ло арши́на два, так что доста́ть её нельзя́ бы́ло и́наче, как вы́пустив из рук верёвку и ма́чту.

Ма́льчик о́чень рассерди́лся и не хоте́л уступи́ть. Он бро́сил ма́чту и ступи́л на перекла́дину. На па́лубе все смотре́ли и смея́лись тому́, что́ выде́лывали обезья́на и капита́нский сын, но как уви́дели, что он пусти́л верёвку и ступи́л на перекла́дину, пока́чивая рука́ми, все за́мерли от стра́ха и мо́лча смотре́ли на него́ и жда́ли, что́ бу́дет.

Вдруг в наро́де кто-то а́хнул от стра́ха. Ма́льчик от э́того кри́ка опо́мнился, гля́нул вниз и зашата́лся.

В э́то вре́мя капита́н корабля́, оте́ц ма́льчика, вы́шел из каю́ты. Он нёс ружьё, чтобы стреля́ть ча́ек. Он увида́л сы́на на ма́чте и то́тчас-же прице́лился в сы́на и закрича́л: ,, В во́ду! Пры́гай сейча́с в во́ду! Застрелю́! `` Ма́льчик шата́лся, но не понима́л. ,, Пры́гай, и́ли застрелю́! Раз, два . . ,`` и как то́лько оте́ц кри́кнул ,, три,`` ма́льчик пры́гнул.

То́чно пу́шечное ядро́, упа́ло те́ло ма́льчика в мо́ре, и не успе́ли во́лны закры́ть его́, как уже́ два́дцать молодцо́в матро́сов спры́гнули с корабля́ в мо́ре. Секу́нд че́рез со́рок—они́ до́лги показа́лись всем—вы́нырнуло те́ло ма́льчика  Его́ схвати́ли и вы́тащили на кора́бль. Че́рез не́сколько мину́т у него́ изо рта́ и из но́са полила́сь вода́, и он стал дыша́ть.

Когда́ капита́н увида́л э́то, он вдруг закрича́л и убежа́л к себе́ в каю́ту, чтобы никто́ не вида́л, как он пла́чет.

## ВОПРО́СЫ

1. Почему́ весь наро́д был на па́лубе?
2. Кто был среди́ люде́й?

3. Как обезьяна забавляла людей на палубе?
4. Кто был мальчик, к которому подпрыгнула обезьяна?
5. Что сделала обезьяна, когда сорвала с мальчика шляпу?
6. Что делала обезьяна со шляпой мальчика?
7. Что сделал мальчик?
8. Что сделали матросы, когда они увидели, что сделала обезьяна?
9. Что сделал мальчик потом?
10. Куда обезьяна повесила шляпу?
11. Что она сделала потом?
12. Можно ли было достать шляпу, не выпуская из рук верёвки и мачты?
13. Как почувствовали себя люди на палубе, увидя как мальчик ступил на перекладину?
14. Что сделал мальчик, когда он услыхал крик?
15. Откуда вышел капитан?
16. Что он нёс в руке, зачем?
17. Что он увидел?
18. Что он велел мальчику?
19. Послушался ли мальчик отца?
20. Что сделали матросы, когда мальчик упал в воду?
21. Что они сделали, когда тело мальчика вынырнуло?
22. Что случилось с мальчиком, когда его положили на палубу?
23. Почему капитан убежал к себе в каюту?

# ПУТЕШЕСТВИЕ ПО ВОЛГЕ

## Глава 1-ая

Мы только что окончили школу, мне было семнадцать лет. Через два месяца я буду студенткой Московского Университета. Какая радость! Сколько впереди интересной работы! А теперь два месяца отдыха, которые надо провести как можно лучше и хорошо отдохнуть. Последний месяц мы очень много работали, так как хотелось кончить школу с отличием.

Мы до́лго ду́мали, что́ нам предприня́ть и наконе́ц реши́ли пое́хать по Во́лге

Я никогда́ ещё не путеше́ствовала да́льше ближа́йших к Москве́ мест, где мы проводи́ли ле́тние кани́кулы, и поэ́тому я осо́бенно была́ ра́да, что мы пое́дем так далёко. Мы должны́ бы́ли дое́хать до Го́рького, бы́вшего Ни́жнего Но́вгорода, по желе́зной доро́ге, а отту́да парохо́дом до А́страхани, го́рода, кото́рый стои́т при впаде́нии Во́лги в Каспи́йское мо́ре.

В Го́рький мы прие́хали ра́но у́тром, парохо́д отходи́л в 12 часо́в, у нас бы́ло доста́точно вре́мени, чтобы осмотре́ть го́род.

В го́роде мно́го стари́нных церкве́й и зда́ний, кото́рые нам хоте́лось уви́деть. Мы подняли́сь на высо́кую го́ру, где нахо́дится стари́нный Кремль, и пе́ред на́ми откры́лся замеча́тельный вид.

Внизу́ шуме́л го́род с его́ бесчи́сленными фа́бриками (Го́рький—центр мануфакту́рной и желе́зной промы́шленности)—автомоби́лями, грузовика́ми, трамва́ями, авто́бусами, пешехо́дами. Всё это шуме́ло, дви́галось, спеши́ло. А пода́льше видне́лась Во́лга, у при́стани стоя́ли парохо́ды, а за при́станью, на друго́м, низово́м берегу́ сине́ли леса́.

Когда́ я уви́дела Во́лгу, э́ту чуде́сную ре́ку с её краси́выми и в э́той ча́сти леси́стыми берега́ми, широ́кую, споко́йную и приво́льную, я чуть не запла́кала от восто́рга. Так вот какова́ она́—на́ша Во́лга!—Мы до́лго сиде́ли на верху́ э́той горы́, на бульва́ре, и не могли́ оторва́ть на́ших взо́ров [1] от необыкнове́нной красоты́ открыва́ющегося пе́ред на́ми ви́да.

[1] To take our eyes off.   оторва́ть, perf. of отрыва́ть = to tear away.

## ВОПРО́СЫ

### Глава́ 1-ая

1. Ско́лько мне бы́ло лет, когда́ я око́нчила шко́лу?
2. Где я собира́лась быть студе́нткой?

 3. Куда́ мы реши́ли пое́хать во вре́мя кани́кул?
 4. Как мы дое́хали до Го́рького?
 5. Как называ́лся пре́жде э́тот го́род?
 6. Где нахо́дится стари́нный Кремль Го́рького?
 7. Како́й центр Го́рький?
 8. Опиши́те вид Во́лги с бульва́ра горы́.
 9. Почему́ мы так до́лго сиде́ли на верху́ горы́?
10. Где нахо́дится А́страхань?   Как мы пое́хали туда́?


## Глава́ 2-а́я

Наконе́ц мы сошли́ вниз и пое́хали на при́стань. Здесь нас уже́ ждал парохо́д. Э́то был прекра́сный, бе́лый, не осо́бенно большо́й, пассажи́рский, двухэта́жный парохо́д. Внизу́ был трюм, ку́хня и каю́ты тре́тьего кла́сса. Наверху́ пе́рвый и второ́й кла́ссы. Всё бы́ло бе́лое, чи́стое, краси́вое и удо́бное. Мы е́хали вторы́м кла́ссом, так как на́ша пое́здка должна́ была́ продолжа́ться о́коло двух неде́ль, и бы́ло бы до́рого е́хать пе́рвым. У нас была́ каю́та на трои́х, в ней то́же всё бы́ло бе́лое. О́кна выходи́ли на па́лубу-вера́нду, кото́рая шла круго́м всего́ парохо́да.

На вера́нде стоя́ли сто́лики и скаме́йки, за э́тими сто́ли-ками в хоро́шую пого́ду пассажи́ры за́втракали, обе́дали, пи́ли чай, у́жинали. На парохо́де была́ та́кже и о́бщая столо́вая, но кто мог сиде́ть в ду́шной ко́мнате, когда́ на во́здухе [1] бы́ло так прекра́сно!

Нам повезло́,[2] пого́да стоя́ла чуде́сная,[3] кака́я быва́ет то́лько в центра́льной Росси́и ле́том: ро́вная, ти́хая, когда́ жа́рко на со́лнце и прохла́дно в тени́, когда́ но́чи коротки́ и благоуха́нны. Така́я пого́да продолжа́ется обыкнове́нно о́коло трёх ме́сяцев—ию́нь, ию́ль и а́вгуст, и́зредка прерыва́ясь гро́зами или недо́лгими дождя́ми, освежа́ющими во́здух. Набежи́т отку́да-нибу́дь ту́чка и

---

[1] Outside, in the fresh air.
[2] We were very lucky.   мне везёт: I am lucky.
[3] The weather was marvellous.

вы́льется сра́зу оби́льным дождём на поля́ и луга́.  На реке́ в таки́е жа́ркие дни осо́бенно прия́тно, с неё ду́ет лёгкий ветеро́к и умеря́ет жар.

Придя́ в на́шу каю́ту мы разложи́ли ве́щи и усе́лись на па́лубе любова́ться Во́лгой.

А любова́ться бы́ло чем [1]—мы плы́ли ми́мо живопи́сных берего́в, покры́тых то ле́сом, то луга́ми, здесь и там видне́лись дере́вни;  на ма́леньких при́станях нас встреча́ли крестья́нки с кувши́нами густо́го парно́го молока́ и с корзи́ночками све́жих я́год пря́мо из ле́са—земляни́ки и мали́ны, кото́рых так мно́го быва́ет в лесу́ в э́то вре́мя го́да. Пассажи́ры покупа́ли и наслажда́лись, так всё бы́ло свежо́, вку́сно, аппети́тно.

К ве́черу посвеже́ло, пассажи́ры рассе́лись на па́лубе, ра́дио передава́ло симфони́ческий конце́рт из Москвы́. Э́то была́ удиви́тельная ночь;  на тёмно-си́нем не́бе мириа́ды звёзд блесте́ли как больши́е бриллиа́нты и отража́лись в Во́лге;  вода́ ти́хо журча́ла под кормо́й, с бе́рега доноси́лось вре́мя от вре́мени пе́ние соловьёв, кото́рых так мно́го в во́лжских леса́х;  из ле́са, с поле́й, из сте́пи доноси́лся не́жный и сла́дкий за́пах ди́ких цвето́в и трав, кото́рый быва́ет то́лько в ру́сских степя́х.  И нет для ру́сского челове́ка прия́тнее и здорове́е э́того за́паха.

[1] There was plenty to admire.

## ВОПРО́СЫ

### Глава́ 2-а́я

1. Где нас ждал парохо́д?
2. Где был тре́тий класс?  Где второ́й и пе́рвый?
3. Каки́м кла́ссом мы е́хали, и почему́?
4. Кака́я была́ на́ша каю́та?
5. Для чего́ стоя́ли сто́лики и скаме́йки на па́лубе-вера́нде?
6. Кака́я была́ пого́да?
7. Что мы сде́лали, когда́ мы пришли́ в каю́ту?

8. Чем покры́ты берега́ Во́лги о́коло Го́рького?
9  Что продава́ли крестья́нки на при́станях?
10. Что передава́ло ра́дио?
11  Пе́ние како́й пти́цы доноси́лось до нас но́чью?
12  За́пах каки́х трав доноси́лся из сте́пи?

### Глава́ 3-тья

На сле́дующий день мы уви́дели реку́ Ка́му, кото́рая впада́ет в Во́лгу о́коло го́рода Каза́ни.

Ка́ма широка́ и глубока́, течёт среди́ скали́стых берего́в Ура́льских отро́гов, покры́тых сосно́вым ле́сом. Когда́ о́бе реки́ слива́ются, Во́лга стано́вится ши́ре и ещё полне́е, бо́льше бежи́т парохо́дов, и увели́чивается число́ барж и плото́в. У Ку́йбышева (го́рода изве́стного ра́ньше под и́менем Сама́ры) Во́лга де́лает большу́ю  пе́тлю— луку́,[1] кото́рая так и называ́ется Сама́рской Луко́й, её берега́ кру́ты, гори́сты и покры́ты ле́сом. Э́ти го́ры зову́т Жигули́ или Жигулёвские го́ры. Э́то необыкнове́нно живопи́сные места́, мо́жет быть са́мые краси́вые на Во́лге.

Во вре́мя на́шего путеше́ствия нас заста́ла гроза́. Оди́н раз с утра́ заходи́ли по́ небу облачка́, ста́ло ду́шно, и к полу́дню облака́ собрали́сь в ту́чи, не́бо потемне́ло, пронёсся ве́тер, Во́лга заволнова́лась, на́чало пока́чивать парохо́д, приближа́лась гроза́. Вдруг разда́лся отдалён- ный гром, немно́го погодя́ [2] сверкну́ла мо́лния, гром послы́шался бли́же и ча́ще, мо́лния сверка́ла зигза́гами по реке́, во́лны с шу́мом поднима́лись и опуска́лись, нас ста́ло кача́ть сильне́е, и вдруг поли́л дождь, тако́й кру́пный и си́льный, что мы все должны́ бы́ли уйти́ в свои́ каю́ты; мы закры́ли о́кна и с удивле́нием смотре́ли на реку́, то́лько что таку́ю споко́йную, а тепе́рь таку́ю взволно́ванную, сплошь покры́тую пузыря́ми, дождь образова́л се́тку, че́рез кото́-

---

[1] Cf. Вели́кие Лу́ки, so often mentioned during the German invasion of Russia 1941-5; this is the big bend of the river Lovát (Ло́вать), near Pskov.

[2] A little later.

рую нельзя́ бы́ло рассмотре́ть берего́в.  Ста́ло хо́лодно.—
Но вот дождь зати́х, ту́чи пронесли́сь, и из-за них сно́ва
вы́глянуло я́ркое со́лнце, грозы́ как не быва́ло.[1]  Река́
успоко́илась, во́здух стал ещё чи́ще и прозра́чнее, мы
вы́шли на па́лубу и по́лной гру́дью [2] вдыха́ли све́жий
во́здух и за́пах ковыля́ доноси́вшийся до нас из сте́пи.

На пя́тый день мы прие́хали в А́страхань, го́род бо́льше
азиа́тский, чем ру́сский.

Он был осно́ван тата́рами в 14-м ве́ке и был изве́стен под
и́менем ,, Золото́й Орды́.“  В нём до сих пор [3] сохрани́-
лись дре́вние постро́йки;  на у́лицах, в рестора́нах,
магази́нах, осо́бенно на ры́нках—смесь наро́дов : тата́р,
пе́рсов, кавка́зцев, калмы́ков, кирги́зов и ру́сских, смесь
языко́в, костю́мов, а над всем э́тим я́ркое горя́чее со́лнце и
си́нее не́бо !—Незабыва́емая пое́здка !

[1] As if there had been no storm at all.
[2] Literally : With a full breast, i.e. deep into our lungs.
[3] Up to the present time.

# ВОПРО́СЫ

## Глава́ 3-тья

1. Кака́я река́ впада́ет в Во́лгу о́коло Каза́ни?
2. Како́й вид име́ет Во́лга, когда́ э́ти две реки́ слива́ются?
3. Что мо́жно ви́деть и слы́шать во вре́мя грозы́?
4. Что случи́лось с парохо́дом во вре́мя грозы́?
5. Что мы сде́лали, когда́ поли́л дождь?
6. Опиши́те вид реки́ во вре́мя грозы́.
7. Что за го́род А́страхань?
8. На како́й день мы прие́хали туда́?
9. Кем и когда́ был осно́ван э́тот го́род?
10  Как он называ́лся пре́жде?
11. Каки́е наро́дности встреча́ются на у́лицах А́страхани?
12. Что вы зна́ете о тата́рах?

# ENGLISH-RUSSIAN VOCABULARY

NOTE.—The translations given are those suitable to the passages in this book, and are by no means the only renderings.

## A

**able to, to be,** мочь, с- (могу́, мо́жешь, 3 pl. мо́гут; past. мог, могла́, могли́); уме́ть, с-; (know how to).

**abroad,** (motion) за грани́цу; (no motion) за грани́цей.

**about** (concerning), о (prep.).

**about** (approximately), о́коло (gen.).

**achievement,** достиже́ние.

**acquaintance of, to make,** знако́миться с (instr.), по-.

**across,** че́рез (acc.).

**act, to** (in a play), игра́ть, сыгра́ть.

**activity,** де́ятельность (f.).

**actually,** действи́тельно.

**advantage of, to take,** по́льзоваться (instr.), вос-.

**adventure,** приключе́ние.

**advice,** сове́т.

**aeroplane,** самолёт.

**afraid, to be,** боя́ться, по-; (бою́сь, бои́шься).

**after** (conj.), по́сле того́ как.

**after** (prep.), по́сле (gen.), че́рез (acc.).

**afterwards,** по́сле э́тогъ, пото́м.

**again,** опя́ть.

**ago,** тому́ наза́д.

**aimless,** бесце́льный

**air,** во́здух.

**air, in the open,** на чи́стом во́здухе.

**Alexei,** Алексе́й.

**all,** весь, вся, всё; pl. все.

**all the same,** всё-таки.

**ally,** сою́зник.

**almost,** почти́.

**along,** по (dat.).

**already,** уже́.

**also,** то́же.

**alter, to,** изменя́ть, -мени́ть.

**although,** хотя́.

**always,** всегда́.

**a.m.,** утра́.

**amazing,** удиви́тельный.

**America,** Аме́рика.

**amuse, to,** забавля́ть, заба́вить (заба́влю, -а́вишь).

**amusing,** заба́вный.

**ancestor,** пре́док (acc. and gen. пре́дка, dat. пре́дку, etc.).

**angry, to get,** серди́ться, рас- ; (сержу́сь, се́рдишься).

**animal,** живо́тное.

**another,** друго́й.

  ,, **one another,** друг-дру́га (the second part only is declined).

**answer, to,** отвеча́ть, отве́тить; (отве́чу, -е́тишь), a person : dative ; a question or letter : на + acc.

**appear, to,** явля́ться, яви́ться (явлю́сь, я́вишься).

**April,** апре́ль (m.).

**arm,** рука́ (see " hand ").

**arm-chair,** кре́сло.

**army,** а́рмия, во́йско

**arrive, to,** приходи́ть, прийти́ (приду́, придёшь); приезжа́ть, прие́хать. (See " go.")

as, как; (when) когда́.
as (because), так как.
as . . . as, так . . . как.
ask, to, (question) спра́шивать, спроси́ть (спрошу́, спро́сишь); (request) проси́ть, по- (прошу́, про́сишь).
asleep, to be, спать (сплю, спишь).
assistant (shop), прика́зчик.
at, у (gen.), в (prep.)
Atlantic, the, Атланти́ческий океа́н.
attention, to pay, обраща́ть, обрати́ть внима́ние (обращу́, обрати́шь).
attractive, привлека́тельный.
aunt, тётя.
author, писа́тель, а́втор.


# B

bag (paper), паке́т.
bare, го́лый.
basket, корзи́на.
bathe, to, купа́ться, вы́-.
bathroom, ва́нная.
beak, клюв.
beautiful, краси́вый.
because, потому́ что.
because of, из-за (gen.).
become, to, станови́ться (становлю́сь, -о́вишься), стать (ста́ну, ста́нешь); generally with instrumental or adverb.
bed, посте́ль (f.), крова́ть (f.).
bedroom, спа́льня (gen. plur. спа́лен).
beer, пи́во.
before (conj.), прежде чем + infin. or indic.; (prep.), до (gen.); пе́ред (instr.).
begin, to, начина́ть, нача́ть (начну́, начнёшь).
beginning, нача́ло.

behind, за (acc. or instr.).
bell, to ring the, звони́ть, по-; (звоню́, звони́шь).
benefit, вы́года.
besides, кро́ме (gen.).
better, лу́чше.
between, ме́жду (instr.).
bicycle, велосипе́д.
big, большо́й.
birch, берёза.
bird, пти́ца.
birthday, рожде́ние.
bit, a, немно́го, немно́жко.
black, чёрный.
blouse, блу́за.
blue, си́ний, -яя, -ее.
board, on, (motion) на парохо́д; (no motion) на парохо́де.
boat, ло́дка, (steamer) парохо́д.
bomb, бо́мба.
book, кни́га.
bookshop, кни́жный магази́н.
born, to be, рожда́ться, роди́ться (рожу́сь, роди́шься).
both, о́ба, fem. о́бе.
both . . . and, как . . . так и.
box (driver's), ко́злы (pl.; gen. ко́зел).
boy, ма́льчик.
branch, ветвь (f.).
break, to, лома́ть, с-; (plants) по́ртить, ис- (по́рчу, по́ртишь).
breakfast, за́втрак.
   „   to have, за́втракать, по-.
bridge, мост.
brightly, я́рко.
bring, to, приноси́ть (-ношу́, но́сишь), принести́ (-несу́, -несёшь; past: -нёс, -ла́, -ли́).
brother, брат, pl. бра́тья, бра́тьев.
build, to, стро́ить, по-.
bus, о́мнибус, автобус.
business, де́ло.
but, но, а.

**buy, to,** покупа́ть, купи́ть (куплю́, ку́пишь).

**by the way,** ме́жду про́чим.

## C

**call for, to,** заходи́ть (-хожу́, -хо́дишь), зайти́, за + instr. (for conj., see " go.")

**called, to be,** называ́ться.

**calm** (of sea) ти́хий.

**camera,** ко́дак.

**can.** (See " able, to be.")

**Canada,** Кана́да.

**capital,** столи́ца.

**car,** автомоби́ль (m.).

**carry, to,** носи́ть (ношу́, но́сишь), нести́ (несу́, несёшь; past: нёс, несла́, -ли́); pf. понести́.

**cart,** теле́га.

**case** (suit) чемода́н

**cat,** ко́шка.

**catch,** лови́ть (ловлю́, ло́вишь), пойма́ть.

**catch sight of,** ви́деть (ви́жу, ви́дишь), у-.

**cathedral,** собо́р.

**cattle,** скот.

**Central Station,** центра́льная ста́нция.

**centre,** центр, середи́на.

**century,** столе́тие, век.

**certainly,** коне́чно, наве́рно.

**change** (subst.), переме́на; (money), ме́лочь (f.).

**characters** (in play), де́йствующие ли́ца.

**chat** (subst.), бесе́да.

**chat, to,** бесе́довать (бесе́дую, бесе́дуешь), по-.

**cheese,** сыр.

**Cherry Orchard,** Вишнёвый Сад.

**child,** ребёнок (ребёнка, ребёнку, etc.).

**childhood,** де́тство.

**children,** де́ти (дете́й, де́тям, детьми́, де́тях).

**chill, to catch, have a,** простужа́ться, простуди́ться (-стужу́сь, -сту́дишься).

**choose, to,** выбира́ть, вы́брать (вы́беру, вы́берешь).

**church,** це́рковь (f.), (це́ркви, церква́м, etc.).

**cigarette,** папиро́са.

**city,** го́род (pl. города́).

**class,** класс.

**class-room,** кла́ссная ко́мната, класс.

**clean,** чи́стый.

**clear,** я́сный.

**clear the table, to,** убира́ть, убра́ть со стола́ (уберу́, уберёшь).

**coal,** у́голь (угля́, углю́, etc.).

**coat,** пальто́ (indecl.).

**coffee,** ко́фе (indecl.).

**cold,** холо́дный; adv. хо́лодно.

**cold, to catch a.** (See " chill.")

**come, to,** приходи́ть, прийти́; приезжа́ть, прие́хать (for conj., see " go.").

**come back, to,** возвраща́ться, возврати́тья (возвращу́сь, -врати́шься); or верну́ться (pf. only), верну́сь, вернёшься.

**come in, to,** входи́ть, войти́ (войду́, войдёшь). (See " go.")

**come up, to,** (piece 33), выходи́ть.

**comfortable,** удо́бный.

**comic,** коми́ческий.

**compare, to,** сра́внивать, сравни́ть.

**completely,** соверше́нно.

**concert,** конце́рт.

**concert-hall,** конце́ртный зал.

**contain, to,** содержа́ть (-держу́, де́ржишь). " It contains " may be rendered by " in it is (or are)."

**continue, to,** продолжа́ть, продо́лжить (-до́лжу, -ишь).

**convenient,** удобный.

**correspond with, to,** переписываться с (instr.).

**correspondent,** корреспондент.

**cost, to,** стоить.

**cottage,** домик.

**country,** (opp. to town) деревня; (geographical term) страна.

**countryside,** пейзаж, деревня.

**couple of hours, a,** часа два.

**course, of,** конечно.

**cousin,** двоюродный брат (pl. братья, братьев).

**cover, to,** покрывать, покрыть (-крою, -кроешь).

**cow,** корова.

**crockery,** посуда.

**cross, to,** переходить, -йти, -ехать, etc., через (acc.). (See " go.")

**crowd,** толпа.

**crowded,** переполненный.

**cruel,** жестокий.

**cup,** чашка.

**customs office,** таможня.

**customs officer,** таможенный чиновник.

**cut (hay), to,** косить, с- (кошу, косишь).

## D

**dance about, to,** танцовать, по-; танцую, -уешь.

**dark,** тёмный; adv. темно.

**darkness falls,** смеркается.

**daughter,** дочь. (See " mother.")

**day,** день (дня).

**day after to-morrow,** послезавтра.

**dead,** мёртвый.

**deal, a good,** много.

**dear,** дорогой.

**decide, to,** решать, решить.

**deck,** палуба.

**deep,** глубокий.

**delicious,** вкусный.

**dense,** густой.

**detective-film,** детективный фильм.

**developed,** развитый.

**dictionary,** словарь (m.) .

**die, to,** умирать, умереть (умру, -рёшь; past: умер, -ла, -ли).

**difference,** разница.

**different from,** непохожий на + acc.

**difficult,** трудный.

**dining-room,** столовая.

**dinner,** обед.

**dirty,** грязный.

**discuss, to,** обсуждать, обсудить (-сужу, -судишь).

**disgraceful,** позорный.

**do, to,** делать, с-.

**doctor,** доктор (pl. доктора).

**dog,** собака.

**doll,** кукла.

**donkey,** осёл (осла, etc.).

**door,** дверь (f.).

**draw, to,** тянуть, по- (тяну, тянешь).

**dream of, to,** (piece 35) представлять себе.

**dress** (subst.), платье.

**dress, to,** одевать, одеть (одену, оденешь); also reflex.: одеваться, одеться.

**drive away,** прогонять, -гнать (-гоню, -гонишь). ‑

**driver,** кучер.

**drop, to,** ронять, уронить (уроню, -онишь).

**duck,** утка (gen. plur. уток).

**during,** во время + gen.

**dusty,** пыльный.

## E

**each,** каждый.

**each other,** друг друга, друг другу, etc.

**early,** ра́нний, -яя, -ее; adv. ра́но.

**easy,** лёгкий; adv. легко́.

**e.g.** (See " example.")

**eight,** во́семь.

**elder,** ста́рший.

**element,** элеме́нт, стихи́я

**else.** (See " or.")

**empty,** пусто́й, пусты́нный

**enable, to,** дава́ть, дать возмо́жность. (See " give.")

**end,** коне́ц (конца́).

**end, in the,** наконе́ц.

**end, to** (intrans.), конча́ться, ко́нчиться.

**engine,** локомоти́в.

**engine-driver,** машини́ст.

**England,** А́нглия.

**English,** англи́йский.

**Englishman,** англича́нин (nom. plur. -ча́не, gen. plur. -ча́н).

**enough,** доста́точно (+ gen.).

**episode,** эпизо́д.

**especially,** осо́бенно.

**Europe,** Евро́па.

**even,** да́же.

**even if,** е́сли да́же.

**evening,** ве́чер (plur. вечера́).

**evening, this,** сего́дня ве́чером.

**every,** ка́ждый.

**everyone,** все + plural verb.

**everything,** всё.

**everywhere,** везде́.

**exaggeration,** преувеличе́ние.

**examine (luggage), to,** осма́тривать, осмотре́ть (-трю, -о́тришь).

**example, for,** наприме́р.

**excellent,** отли́чный.

**excited, to become,** волнова́ться. вз-, за-(волну́юсь, -у́ешься).

**exclaim, to,** восклица́ть, воскли́кнуть (-кну, -кнёшь).

**excursion,** пое́здка.

**expensive,** дорого́й.

**eye,** глаз (pl. глаза́, глаз).

**E**

**F**

**face,** лицо́.

**factory,** заво́д, фа́брика (at, in, to: на).

**fairly,** дово́льно.

**family,** семья́ (nom. plur. се́мьи, gen. plur. семе́й).

**far from,** далеко́ от (+ gen.).

**farm,** колхо́з, фе́рма.

**farmer,** колхо́зник, фе́рмер, крестья́нин (pl. -я́не, -я́н).

**fast** (adv.), ско́ро.

**faster,** скоре́е.

**father,** оте́ц (отца́, etc.).

**favourite** (adj.) люби́мый.

**feed, to** (trans.), корми́ть, на-(кормлю́, ко́рмишь).

**feel.** (See " pulse.")

**few, a,** немно́го (gen.).

**few, so,** так ма́ло (gen.).

**few, very,** о́чень ма́ло (gen.).

**field,** по́ле.

**fifty,** пятьдеся́т.

**fight, to,** сража́ться, срази́ться (сражу́сь, срази́шься).

**film,** фи́льм.

**finally,** наконе́ц.

**find, to,** находи́ть, найти́. (See " go.")

**fine,** краси́вый, хоро́ший.

**finish, to,** конча́ть, ко́нчить.

**fire,** ого́нь (огня́, etc.); (fireside), оча́г.

**firm,** фи́рма.

**first,** пе́рвый; (adv.) сперва́, снача́ла.

**fish,** ры́ба.

**five,** пять.

**flag,** флаг.

**flat** (adj.), ро́вный, пло́ский.

**flat** (subst.), кварти́ра.

**floor** (storey), эта́ж.

**flower,** цвето́к (цветка́, pl. цветы́).

**flower-bed,** клу́мба.

**fly, to,** летáть, по- ; (be flying), летéть, по- (лечý, летúшь).

**fly away, to,** улетáть, улетéть (conjug. as above).

**fog,** тумáн.

**follow (advice), to,** слéдовать (слéдую, -дуешь), по- ; + dat.

**fond of, to be,** любúть (люблю́, лю́бишь), по-.

**for** (conj.), так как.

**for** (prep.), для (gen.) ; ва (instr.) with idea of fetching.

**foreign,** инострáнный ; чужóй.

**foreigner,** инострáнец (-áнца, etc.).

**forest,** лес (N.B.: в лесý; plur. лесá).

**forget, to,** забывáть, забы́ть (забýду, забýдешь).

**fortunately,** к счáстью.

**four,** четы́ре.

**fourth,** четвёртый.

**France,** Фрáнция.

**free,** свобóдный.

**freeze over, to,** замерзáть, замёрзнуть (замёрзну, -нешь, past : вамёрз, -мёрзла, -мёрзли).

**French,** францýзский.

**frequently,** чáсто.

**friend,** друг (pl. друзья́, друзéй) ; fem. : подрýга.

**friendly,** дрýжеский.

**friends with, to make,** дружúться, по-, с (instr.).

**frightened,** испýганный.

**frock-coat,** сюртýк.

**from,** от (gen.), из (gen.).

**front, in** (adv.), впередú.

**front of, in,** пéред (instr.).

**front door,** передняя дверь.

**fruit,** фрукт (usually in plural).

**fruit-tree,** фруктóвое дéрево (nom. plur. дерéвья, gen. plur. дерéвьев).

**full of,** пóлный (short form : пóлон, полнá, etc.) + gen.

## G

**game,** игрá.

**garden,** сад (N.B. : в садý).

**gay,** весёлый.

**general, in,** вообщé.

**generally,** обыкновéнно.

**get, to.** (See " become," " buy " or " receive.")

**get out, to** выходúть, вы́йти. (See " go.")

**get to know, to.** (See " acquainted with.")

**get up, to,** вставáть (встаю́, встаёшь), встать (встáну, встáнешь).

**girl,** дéвушка, (little girl) дéвочка (gen. plur. -ек).

**give, to,** давáть (даю́, даёшь), дать (дам, дашь, даст, дадúм, дадúте, дадýт).

**give up, to,** бросáть, брóсить (брóшу, брóсишь).

**glad,** рад, рáда, рáды.

**glass** (of water, beer, etc.), стакáн.

**go, to,** ходúть (хожý, хóдишь), иттú, по- (идý, идёшь ; past : шёл, шла, шли) ; éздить (éзжу, éздишь), éхать, по- (éду, éдешь).

**go away, to,** уходúть, уйтú (conjug. as above).

**go back, to.** (See " come back.")

**go into, to,** входúть, войтú (conjug. as above).

**go out, to,** выходúть, вы́йти (conjug. as above).

**go up to, to,** подходúть, подойтú к (dat.).

**goat,** козёл (козлá, etc.).

**good,** хорóший.

**good-bye,** до свидáния !

**Gothic,** готúческий.

**gradually,** мáло-по-мáлу, постепéнно.

**great,** большóй.

**green**, зелёный.
**greetings**, привет.
**grey**, серый.
**ground**, земля (асс. землю).
**guard** (railway), кондуктор (plur. -а).
**gun** (cannon), орудие.

## H

**half an hour**, полчаса (gen. получаса, etc.).
**hall** (of house), передняя.
**hand**, рука (асс. руку ; pl. руки).
**handkerchief**, платок (платка, etc.).
**happen, to**, случаться, случиться.
**happy**, счастливый (pred. form : счастлив).
**harbour**, гавань (f.), порт.
**hard** (of work), тяжёлый.
**harvest**, жатва, урожай.
**hat**, шляпа.
**have to, I ; we**, я должен, -жна ; мы должны.
**hay**, сено.
**he**, он.
**headache, I have a**, у меня болит голова.
**hear, to**, слышать, у- (слышу, -шишь).
**hearty**, сердечный.
**heavy**, тяжёлый.
**help, to**, помогать, помочь (помогу, -можешь, 3rd pl. -могут ; past : помог, -могла, могли). Both verbs govern the dative.
**her**, её (асс. and gen. ; also possessive).
**here**, здесь ; (hither) сюда.
**high**, высокий ; adv. высоко.
**him**, его (асс. and gen.).
**his**, его.
**Hitler troops**, гитлеровские войска.

**hole** (piece 33), отверстие.
**home**, дом ; (homewards) домой.
**home, at**, дома.
**hope, to**, надеяться, по-.
**horrible**, ужасный.
**horse**, лошадь (f.).
**horseback, on**, верхом.
**horse-cab**, дрожки.
**hospital**, больница.
**hour** (see also " half "), час.
**hour and a half, an**, полтора часа.
**house**, дом (pl. дома, домов, etc.).
**however**, однако.
**how much**, сколько (gen.).
**hundred**, сто.
**hungry**, голодный.
**hurry, to**, спешать (спешу, -йшь), по-.
**husband**, муж (pl. мужья, мужей).

## I

**I**, я.
**if**, если.
**imagine**, воображать, вообразить (воображу, -разишь).
**immediately**, сейчас-же.
**important**, важный.
**impossible**, невозможный.
**impression, to produce on**, производить (-вожу, -водишь), произвести впечатление на + асс. (-веду, -ведёшь, past : -вёл, -вела, -вели).
**in, into**, в (асс. and prep.).
**increase, to** (intrans.), увеличиваться, увеличиться.
**inn**, трактир.
**innumerable**, бесчисленный.
**interested in, to be**, интересоваться, за- + instr. (-суюсь, -суешься).
**interesting**, интересный.
**introduce, to**, знакомить, по-, с + instr. (знакомлю, -омишь).

invent, to, изобретать, изобрести (-брету, -бретёшь, past: -брёл, -брела, -брели).

invite, to, приглашать, пригласить (-глашу, -гласишь).

## J

jacket, куртка.
job, место.
John, Иван.
jolly, весёлый.
July, июль (m.).
jump down from, to, соскакивать, соскочить, с + gen. (-кочу, -кочишь).
jump up, to, вскакивать, вскочить.

## K

kid-gloves, лайковые перчатки.
kiss, to, целовать, по- (целую, -уешь).
kitchen, кухня.
knit, to, вязать, с- (вяжу, вяжешь).
know, to, знать, у-.
knowledge, знание.

## L

lady, дама.
lake, озеро (pl. озёра, озёр, etc.).
lane, переулок, тропинка.
language, язык.
large, большой.
lark, жаворонок (жаворонка, etc.).
last (see also "week," "year"), последний, -яя, -ее; прошлый.
last, at, наконец.
last, to, продолжаться, продолжиться (see "continue").

late (adv.), поздно.
late, to be late at, опаздывать, опоздать, к + dat. or на + acc.
later (adv.), спустя.
laugh at, to, смеяться, за-, над + instr. (смеюсь, смеёшься).
lawn, лужайка.
lawyer, адвокат.
lay the table, to, накрывать, накрыть на стол (-крою, -кроешь).
lead, водить (вожу, водишь), вести, по- (веду, ведёшь, past: вёл, вела, вели).
lead a life, to, вести образ жизни, по- (conjug. as above).
leaf, лист (pl. листья, листьев, etc.).
learn, to, учиться, вы- (учусь, учишься); the thing learnt goes into the dative.
least, at, по крайней мере.
leave, to (intrans.), (see "go away"); (of train) отходить, отойти.
leave, to (trans.), выходить, выйти из (gen.); оставлять, оставить (оставлю, -авишь), (school) кончать, кончить.
lecture, лекция (to, at: на).
lesson, урок.
let, to (allow), позволять, позволить (-волю, -волишь; imperat. позволь, -вольте).
letter, письмо.
lick, to, лизать, по- (лижу, лижешь).
lie, to, лежать, по- (лежу, -ишь).
life, жизнь (f.).
light (adj.), светлый.
like, как.
like, to, любить, по- (люблю, любишь).
like, I should, я бы хотел, мне хочется.

lines (railway), рельсы.
listen, to, слушать, по-.
little, маленький.
little, a, немного.
little way, a, немного.
live, to, жить, по- (живу, живёшь).
London (adj.), лондонский.
Londoner, житель Лондона.
lonely, to be, скучать, по-.
long (adj.), длинный.
long (adv.), давно, долго (for a long time).
look at, to, смотреть, по-, на + acc. (смотрю, смотришь).
look for, to, искать, по- (ищу, ищешь).
look out of, to, смотреть в (acc.). (See " look at.")
look out on to, to, выходить на (acc.).
lorry, грузовик.
lose sight of, to, терять, по-, из виду.
lot, a (of), много (gen.).
loud, громкий.
lovely, прекрасный.
luggage, багаж.
lunch (subst.), завтрак.
lunch, to have, завтракать, по-.

# M

machine, машина.
macintosh, макинтош.
magnificent, великолепный.
main road, большая дорога.
make, to, делать, с-; (compel) заставлять, заставить (заставлю, -ставишь).
man, мужчина (m.); (human) человек.
mankind, человечество.
manner of life, образ жизни.
mantle, покров.

many, много (gen.).
many, a good, довольно много (gen.).
many, so, так много (gen.).
market, рынок (рынка, etc., in : на).
marry, to (of the man), жениться на + prepositional.
master, хозяин (pl. хозяева).
meadow, луг (sing. луга, etc.; pl. луга).
meat, мясо.
medical, медицинский.
meet, to, встречать, встретить (встречу, встретишь); (make acquaintance of, see " acquaintance ").
melt, to, таять, рас-.
merry, весёлый.
Michael, Михаил.
middle of, in the, среди (gen.).
midnight, полночь (gen. полуночи).
minute, минута.
modern, современный.
moment, момент, мгновение.
money, деньги (pl. only ; gen. денег).
monkey, обезьяна.
month, месяц.
more, больше (gen.).
morning, утро.
    ,,    good, здравствуйте !
    ,,    in the, утром.
Moscow, Москва.
Moscow Art Theatre, Московский Художественный Театр.
most of, большинство из (gen.).
mother, мать (acc. мать, gen., dat., prep. матери, instr. матерью, pl. матери, матерей, матерям, etc.)
motor-car, автомобиль (m.).
mountain, гора (nom. and acc. plur. горы, dat. горам, etc.).
movement, движение.

**much,** мно́го (gen.).
**mushroom,** гриб (гриба́, etc.).
**music,** му́зыка.
**must,** до́лжен, должна́, должно́,
    должны́ + infin.
**must not,** нельзя́ + dat. and infin.
**my,** мой, моя́, моё, мои́.


## N

**native** (adj.), родно́й.
**natural,** натура́льный, есте́ствен-
    ный, просто́й (piece 30).
**near,** о́коло (gen.), бли́зко от
    (gen.), недалеко́ от (gen.).
**nearly,** почти́.
**need, I,** render by: мне ну́жен,
    нужна́, ну́жно, нужны́.
**needlework, to do,** шить, с- ; (шью,
    шьёшь.)
**neighbour,** сосе́д (plur. сосе́ди,
    gen. сосе́дей.)
**neighbourhood,** окре́стность (f.).
**nest,** гнездо́ (plur. гнёзда).
**never,** никогда́.
**new,** но́вый.
**newspaper,** газе́та.
**next,** бу́дущий, сле́дующий.
**nice** (friendly), любе́зный.
**Nicholas,** Никола́й.
**noise,** шум.
**noisy,** шу́мный.
**no,** нет.
**no one,** никто́.
**north** (wards), к се́веру.
**northern,** се́верный.
**not,** не.
**not far from,** недалеко́ от (gen.).
**not yet,** ещё не, ещё нет.
**note** (money), бума́жка.
**nothing,** ничто́, ничего́.
**now,** тепе́рь.
**now-a-days,** в на́ше вре́мя.
**number,** число́.
**nut,** оре́х.


## O

**of course,** коне́чно.
**office,** конто́ра.
**often,** ча́сто.
**old,** ста́рый.
**old man,** стари́к.
**old woman,** стару́ха.
**older,** ста́рше.
**omnibus,** о́мнибус, авто́бус.
**on,** на (acc. and prep.).
**once,** раз, одна́жды.
**once, at,** сейча́с-же.
**one,** оди́н, одна́, одно́.
**one day,** (past) одна́жды ; (future)
    когда́-нибудь.
**only,** то́лько.
**open** (adj.), откры́тый.
**open, to,** открыва́ть, откры́ть,
    (откро́ю, -кро́ешь).
**open air.** (See " air.")
**opera,** о́пера.
**operation,** опера́ция.
**opposite,** про́тив (gen.).
**or,** и́ли.
**or else,** и́ли же.
**order, to** (something), зака́зы-
    вать,    заказа́ть    (-кажу́,
    -ка́жешь).
**order to, in,** что́бы + infin.
**ordinary,** обыкнове́нный.
**other,** друго́й.
**our,** наш.
**out of,** из (gen.).
**out-of-doors,** на дворе́.
**overcoat,** пальто́ (indecl.).
**own** (adj.), со́бственный.


## P

**parcel,** паке́т.
**parents,** роди́тели(роди́телей,etc.).
**Paris,** Пари́ж.
**park,** парк.
**part** (in a play), роль (f.).

**particular**, осо́бенный.
**pass, to**, ходи́ть, итти́, е́хать, etc., ми́мо (gen.).
**pass through to**, проходи́ть, etc., че́рез (acc.).
**passenger**, пассажи́р.
**past**, ми́мо (gen.).
**path**, тропи́нка.
**patient** (subst.) пацие́нт.
**pavement**, тротуа́р.
**peace**, мир.
**peasant**, крестья́нин (nom. plur. -я́не, gen. -я́н).
**people**, лю́ди (люде́й, лю́дям, людьми́, лю́дях)
**people, a lot of**, мно́го наро́ду.
**perform, to**, (operation) де́лать, с-; (in theatre) игра́ть, сыгра́ть.
**performance**, представле́ние, постано́вка.
**pet**, люби́мец (люби́мца, etc.).
**Peter**, Пётр (Петра́, etc.).
**pick up, to**, поднима́ть, подня́ть (подниму́, -и́мешь).
**picture**, карти́нка.
**picturesque**, живопи́сный.
**piece**, кусо́к (куска́, etc.).
**pine**, сосна́.
**pipe**, тру́бка; (instrument) фле́йта.
**plant** (subst.), расте́ние.
**plant, to**, сажа́ть, посади́ть (-сажу́, -са́дишь)
**platform**, платфо́рма.
**play** (subst.), пье́са.
**play, to**, (game) игра́ть, сыгра́ть, в (acc.); (instrument) игра́ть, сыгра́ть на (prep.).
**pleasant**, прия́тный.
**please**, пожа́луйста.
**please, to**, нра́виться, по- (dat.); I like, мне нра́вится.
**pleasure**, удово́льствие.
**pocket**, карма́н.
**polite**, ве́жливый.

**pond**, пруд (N.B. в, на пруду́).
**poor**, бе́дный.
**poplar**, то́поль (m.).
**port**, порт.
**porter**, носи́льщик.
**possible**, возмо́жный.
**postcard**, откры́тка.
**postman**, почтальо́н.
**post-office**, по́чта (at, in, to: на).
**prairie**, степь.
**prefer, to**, предпочита́ть, предпоче́сть (-почту́, -почтёшь).
**pretty**, краси́вый, хоро́шенький.
**probably**, вероя́тно.
**produce, to** (a play), ста́вить, по- (ста́влю, ста́вишь).
**professor**, профе́ссор (nom. plur. -а́).
**progress, to make**, де́лать успе́хи, с-.
**pronunciation**, произноше́ние.
**protect, to**, защища́ть, защити́ть (-ищу́, -ити́шь).
**proud**, го́рдый.
**proud of, to be**, горди́ться (instr.) (горжу́сь, -ди́шься).
**pulse, to feel**, щу́пать пульс, по-.
**pupil**, учени́к.
**put, to** (place, lay), класть (кладу́, -дёшь), положи́ть (положу́, -ло́жишь).
**put into, to** (hand into pocket), сова́ть (сую́, суёшь), су́нуть, в (acc.) (су́ну, -нешь).
**put on, to**, надева́ть, наде́ть (наде́ну, -де́нешь).

**Q**

**quay**, набережная.
**question**, вопро́с.
**question, to ask a**, задава́ть, зада́ть вопро́с (for conjugation, see " give ").
**quickly**, бы́стро, ско́ро.

**quiet,** тихий.

**quite** (completely), совершённо; (fairly) довóльно.

## R

**radio,** рáдио.

**railway,** желéзная дорóга.

**raining, it is,** идёт дождь (m.).

**rather** (a bit), немнóго; (would rather: see " prefer ").

**reach, to,** доходи́ть, дойти́, доéхать до (gen.), (see " go ").

**read, to,** читáть, про- or прочéсть (-чту́, -чтёшь; past: -чёл, -члá, -чли́).

**ready,** готóвый.

**real,** настоя́щий.

**realise, to,** понимáть, поня́ть (пойму́, -мёшь).

**really,** в сáмом дéле.

**receive, to,** получáть, получи́ть (получу́, -лу́чишь).

**recently,** недáвно.

**red,** крáсный.

**Red Army man,** красноармéец (gen. -армéйца).

**red-faced,** красноли́цый.

**relation,** рóдственник, fem. -венница.

**remain,** оставáться (остаю́сь, -ёшься), остáться (остáнусь, -нешься)

**remember, to,** пóмнить, вс-.

**replace, to,** замещáть, замести́ть (-мещу́, -мести́шь).

**reply, to.** (See " answer.")

**represent, to,** изображáть, изобрази́ть (-бражу́, -брази́шь).

**restaurant,** ресторáн.

**rest of, the,** остáток (-тка).

**return, to.** (See " come back.")

**ring the bell, to,** звони́ть, по-.

**river,** рекá (acc. рéку, pl. рéки).

**road,** дорóга.

**roof,** кры́ша.

**room,** кóмната.

**rouble,** рубль (m.).

**row,** ряд.

**run, to,** бéгать, по-; (frequentative) бежáть, по- (бегу́, бежи́шь).

**run up to, to,** подбегáть, -бежáть к (dat.)—as above.

**Russia,** Росси́я; (now more usually) Совéтский Сою́з.

**Russian,** русский.

## S

**saddle,** седлó (pl. сёдла, сёдел).

**sailing-ship,** корáбль (m.).

**same,** сáмый, тот же сáмый.

**save, to,** спасáть, спасти́ (спасу́, -сёшь; past: спас. слá, -сли́),

**say, to,** говори́ть, сказáть (скажу́, скáжешь).

**scene** (view), вид.

**school,** шкóла.

**school-friend,** шкóльный товáрищ (fem. -ая подру́га).

**science,** нау́ка.

**sea,** мóре.

**seagull,** чáйка.

**seat** (in bus, theatre, etc.), мéсто.

**second,** вторóй.

**see, to,** ви́деть, у- (ви́жу, ви́дишь).

**seem, to,** казáться, по- (кажу́сь, кáжешься).

**seize, to,** хватáть, схвати́ть (схвачу́, -áтишь).

**sell, to,** продавáть, продáть (for conjugation, see " give ").

**send, to,** посылáть, послáть (пошлю́. -шлёшь).

**Sergei,** Сергéй.

**service,** слу́жба.

**set off for, to,** отправля́ться, отпрáвиться, к (dat.), в or на (acc.) (отпрáвлюсь, -áвишься).

**seven, семь.**

several, не́сколько (gen.).
sheep, овца́ (gen. plur. ове́ц).
shine, to, сия́ть, за-.
shirt, руба́шка.
shoe, башма́к.
shop, магази́н, ла́вка.
shopping, to go, де́лать поку́пки, с-.
shortly, вско́ре.
short story, расска́з.
shoulder, плечо́ (nom. plur. пле́чи).
shout, to, крича́ть, за-.
show, to, пока́зывать, показа́ть (-кажу́, -ка́жешь).
sick, больно́й.
sing, to, петь, с- (пою́, поёшь).
sister, сестра́ (nom. plur. сёстры, gen. сестёр).
sit, to, сиде́ть (сижу́, сиди́шь), по-.
sit down, to, сади́ться (сажу́сь, сади́шься), сесть (ся́ду, ся́дешь; past: сел, се́ла, се́ли).
sitting-room, гости́ная.
six, шесть.
skate, ката́ться на конька́х, по-.
skater, конькобе́жец (gen. -бе́жца).
skiing, to go, ката́ться на лы́жах.
skirt, ю́бка.
sledge, to travel on, ката́ться на са́нках.
sleepy, I am, мне хо́чется спать.
slightly, немно́жко.
slowly, ме́дленно.
small, ма́ленький.
smoke (subst.), дым.
smoke, to, кури́ть (курю́, ку́ришь), вы-.
snow, снег.
snowball, снежо́к (снежка́, etc.).
snowman, сне́жная ку́кла.
so, так; (therefore) поэ́тому.
sock, чуло́к (чулка́, etc.).
soldier, солда́т; красноарме́ец (see " Red Army man ").

some, не́сколько (gen.).
some day, когда́-нибу́дь.
someone, кто́-то, кто-нибу́дь.
something, что́-то, что-нибу́дь.
sometimes, иногда́.
son, сын (plur. сыновья́, сынове́й).
song (of birds), пе́ние.
soon, ско́ро, вско́ре.
soon, as soon as, как то́лько.
soon, as soon as possible, как мо́жно скоре́е.
sound, звук.
soup, суп (gen. су́пу).
Soviet Union, Сове́тский Сою́з.
speak, to, говори́ть, по-, сказа́ть (скажу́, ска́жешь).
spend, to (of time), проводи́ть (-вожу́, -во́дишь), провести́ (-веду́, -ведёшь; past: провёл, -вела́, -вели́).
spring, весна́.
stage-coach, дилижа́нс.
stamp, ма́рка.
stamp-album, альбо́м для почто́вых ма́рок.
stand, to, стоя́ть, по- (стою́, стои́шь).
station, ста́нция; (terminus) вокза́л (at, to: на).
stay, to. (See " remain " and " live.")
steam-engine, парово́з.
steamer, парохо́д.
step, шаг.
stick, па́лка.
still, всё, всё ещё.
stop, to (intrans.), остана́вливаться, останови́ться (see below).
stop, to (trans.), остана́вливать, останови́ть (-овлю́, -о́вишь).
stop (subst.), остано́вка.
story, расска́з, анекдо́т.
straight, прямо́й.
street, у́лица.

**study, to,** учи́ться, вы́- (учу́сь, у́чишься); the thing studied goes into the dative.

**suburb,** окра́ина го́рода.

**succeed, to,** удава́ться, уда́ться, impersonal + dat. I succeed: мне удаётся; fut. perf. уда́стся; past: удава́лось, удало́сь.

**suddenly,** вдруг, внеза́пно.

**suffering,** страда́ние.

**summer,** ле́то.

**summer** (adj.), ле́тний, -яя, -ее.

**sun,** со́лнце; in the sun: на со́лнце.

**sure, I am,** я уве́рен, fem. уве́рена.

**surgeon,** хиру́рг.

**surprised, to be,** удивля́ться, удиви́ться (-влю́сь, -ви́шься).

**sweep, to,** мести́, вы́- (мету́, метёшь); past: мёл, -ла́, -ли́).

**swim, to,** пла́вать, по-.

**symphony,** симфо́ния.

### T

**table,** стол.

**take, to,** брать (беру́, берёшь), взять (возьму́, -мёшь).

**take off, to,** снима́ть, снять (сниму́, сни́мешь).

**tale,** расска́з.

**talk, to,** говори́ть, по- (to: с + instr.).

**tall,** высо́кий.

**taxi,** такси́.

**teacher,** учи́тель.

**telegram,** телегра́мма.

**telegraph,** телегра́ф.

**telephone,** телефо́н.

**tell, to,** говори́ть, сказа́ть (скажу́, ска́жешь).

**temperature, to take,** ме́рять температу́ру, по- or с-.

**than,** чем.

**thank, to,** благодари́ть, по- (for: за + acc.).

**that** (conj.), что.

**that** (demonstr.), тот, та, то; pl. те.

**theatre,** теа́тр.

**their,** их (indecl.)

**then,** (next) пото́м; (at that time) тогда́.

**there,** (no motion) там; (motion) туда́.

**thick,** густо́й.

**thing,** вещь (f.).

**think, to,** ду́мать, по-.

**thirsty, I am,** мне пить хо́чется.

**this,** э́тот, э́та, э́то; pl. э́ти.

**three,** три.

**through,** че́рез (acc.), сквозь (acc.).

**Thursday,** четве́рг.

**ticket,** биле́т.

**tie,** га́лстук.

**till,** (conj.) пока́ . . . не; (prep.) до (gen.).

**time,** вре́мя (вре́мени, etc.); (occasion) раз.

**time, for a long,** до́лго, давно́.

**time, from time to time,** вре́мя от вре́мени.

**time, it is time to,** пора́ + infin.

**tiny,** кро́шечный.

**tired, to be or grow,** устава́ть (устаю́, -ёшь); уста́ть (уста́ну, уста́нешь).

**to and fro,** взад и вперёд.

**tobogganing, to go,** ката́ться на сала́зках.

**to-day,** сего́дня; (now-a-days) в на́ше вре́мя.

**together,** вме́сте.

**Tolstoy,** Толсто́й (Толсто́го, etc.).

**too** (also) то́же; (+ adj. or adv.), сли́шком.

**top** (of bus), верх, верху́шка.

**top-hat,** цили́ндр.

**torpedo,** торпе́до.

touch, to (piece 33), каса́ться, косну́ться + gen.
tower, ба́шня.
town, го́род (pl. города́).
toy, игру́шка.
toy-shop, игру́шечная ла́вка.
train, по́езд (pl. поезда́).
tram, трамва́й.
travel, to, е́хать, по- (see " go "); е́здить (е́зжу, е́здишь); (travel afar) путеше́ствовать.
treat, to, обходи́ться, обойти́сь с (instr.) (See " come ").
tree, де́рево (pl. дере́вья, дере́вьев, etc.).
trip, пое́здка.
troops, войска́.
trousers, штаны́.
true, it is, ве́рно.
try, to, стара́ться, по- ; пыта́ться, по-.
tunnel, тунне́ль (m.).
Turgenev, Турге́нев.
twelve, двена́дцать.
twelve, half-past, полови́на пе́рвого.
twice, два ра́за.

## U

Ukraine, the, Украи́на, Укра́йна.
umbrella, зо́нтик.
uncle, дя́дя (decline like feminine noun).
under, под (acc. and instr.).
Underground, the, Метро́.
understand, to, понима́ть, поня́ть (пойму́, -мёшь).
undo, to (a parcel), развя́зывать, развяза́ть (-вяжу́, -вя́жешь).
unexpected, неожи́данный.
unfortunately, к сожале́нию.
unhappy, несча́стный.
university, университе́т.
unpleasant, неприя́тный.

upstairs, (motion) наве́рх ; (no motion) наверху́.
up to, до (gen.).
U.S.A., Соединённые Шта́ты.
use, to, употребля́ть, употреби́ть (-блю́, -би́шь).
U.S.S.R., С.С.С.Р., Сою́з Сове́тских Социалисти́ческих Респу́блик ; Сове́тский Сою́з.

## V

various, ра́зный.
vast, обши́рный.
vegetables, о́вощи.
very, о́чень.
vice versa, наоборо́т.
village, село́ (pl. сёла).
visit, to, навеща́ть, навести́ть (-вещу́, -вести́шь).
visitor, гость (gen. plur. госте́й).
voyage, путеше́ствие.

## W

wait, to, ждать, подо- (gen.) (жду, ждёшь).
wake up, to, просыпа́ться, просну́ться (-сну́сь, -снёшься).
walk, to, (go on foot) ходи́ть, итти́ пешко́м (see " go "); (go for a walk) гуля́ть, по-.
want, to, хоте́ть, за- ; (хочу́, хо́чешь, хоти́м, хотя́т).
war, война́.
warm, тёплый ; I am warm : мне тепло́.
warmer, тепле́е.
wave, to, маха́ть, махну́ть + instr.
way, in this, таки́м о́бразом.
wear, to, носи́ть, по- (ношу́, но́сишь).
weather, пого́да.

**Wednesday,** среда (асс. среду).
**week,** неделя.
**week, last,** на прошлой неделе.
**week, this,** на этой неделе.
**well,** хорошо.
**well-known,** известный.
**wet,** (rainy) дождливый.
**what,** что.
**what a,** что за.
**when, whenever,** когда.
**where,** (no motion) где; (motion) куда.
**which,** (interrog.) какой; (rel.) который.
**while,** в то время, как.
**whistle,** свист.
**white,** белый.
**who,** (interrog.) кто; (rel.) который.
**whole,** весь, вся, всё, все.
**why,** почему.
**widow,** вдова.
**wife,** жена (pl. жёны).
**window,** окно (pl. окна, gen. окон).
**winter,** зима (асс. зиму).
**winter (adj.),** зимний, -яя, -ее.

**wish, to,** желать, по- (gen.).
**with,** с (instr.); often plain instrumental.
**woman,** женщина.
**wonderful,** чудный, удивительный.
**wood,** лес (nom. plur. леса).
**wooden,** деревянный.
**work (subst.),** работа.
**work, to,** работать, по-.
**worry, to,** беспокоиться, за-.
**write, to,** писать, на- (пишу, пишешь).
**writer,** писатель (m.).

## Y

**year,** год.
**year, last,** в прошлом году.
**year, next,** в будущем году.
**year, this,** в этом году.
**yellow,** жёлтый.
**yes,** да.
**yesterday,** вчера.
**yet,** (time) ещё; (however) всё-таки, однако.

# RUSSIAN-ENGLISH VOCABULARY

(See note on page 61.)

## A

áвгуст, August.
автóбус, motor-bus.
автомобиль (m.), motor-car.
азиáтский, Asiatic.
амбáр, barn.
áнгел, angel.
аппетитный, appetising.
áрка, arch.
аромáт, perfume, scent.
аршин, arshin (28 inches).
ах!, ah! oh!
áхать, áхнуть, to say ah! to
   groan.

## Б

банк, bank (for money).
бáтюшка, (little) father, papa;
  бáтюшки мой! : Good Heavens!
башмáк, shoe.
бéдный, poor.
бежáть, по- (бегý, бежишь, бегýт)
  бéгать, по- (frequentative), to
  run.
белéться, за-, to appear white.
бéлый, white.
бéрег (nom. pl. берегá), bank,
  shore.
бесéдка, summer-house.
бесéдовать, по- (-сéдую, -дуешь),
  to chat.
бесчисленный, countless.
благодáть (f.), blessing, abund-
ance.

благоухáнный, fragrant.
блéдный, pale.
блестéть, за- (блещý, блестишь),
  to shine, glitter.
блестящий, bright, shining.
ближáйший. (See близкий.)
ближе. (See близкий.)
близкий, near; (compar. ближе,
  superl. ближáйший).
блýзка, blouse.
блюдо, dish, course.
бóдрый, sound, healthy.
боковóй, side (adj.), by-.
болéть, за-, to be ill, fall ill.
болтáть по-, to chatter, gossip.
больница, hospital.
больнóй, sick, ill; (as noun)
  patient.
бóльше, more.
бóльшею чáстью, for the most
  part.
бóльший, bigger, larger.
большóй, big, large.
бóтик, over-shoe.
бранить, по-, to scold, rebuke.
брат (nom. pl. брáтья, gen.
  брáтьев), brother.
брать (берý, берёшь); взять
  (возьмý, -мёшь), to take.
бриллиáнт, diamond.
бросáть, брóсить (брóшу, брóсишь), to throw, throw down,
  give up, abandon.
бросáться, брóситься (conjug. as
  above), to rush.
будить, раз- (бужý, бýдишь),
  to awaken, rouse.

77

**бу́дничный**, work-day (adj.).

**бу́лка**, white loaf, roll, bun.

**бульва́р**, boulevard.

**буфе́т**, sideboard.

**буфе́тная**, pantry.

**бы**, particle expressing conditional or subjunctive.

**быва́ть**, to be (usually), visit, happen.

**бы́вший**, former.

**бы́стрый**, swift.

**быть**, to be.

## В

**в, во** (acc. and prep.), in, into.

**ва́жный**, important.

**ва́за**, vase.

**варе́нье**, jam.

**Ва́ся** (dimin. of **Васи́лий**), Basil.

**ваш, ва́ша, ва́ше,** pl. **ва́ши,** your.

**вдоль** (gen.), along.

**вдруг**, suddenly.

**вдыха́ть, вдохну́ть**, to breathe in.

**везде́**, everywhere.

**везти́, по-** (везу́, везёшь; past: вёз, везла́, -ли́), to convey, transport, carry.

**мне везёт**, I am lucky.

**век** (pl. века́ and ве́ки), century.

**веле́ть, по-** (велю́, -ли́шь), to order, command.

**вели́кий**, great.

**вера́нда**, veranda.

**верёвка**, cord, string.

**ве́рно**, really, truly.

**верте́ться, по-** (верчу́сь, ве́ртишься), to turn, turn round.

**верх**, top.

**весели́ть, раз-**, to cheer, make merry.

**весёлый**, gay, cheerful, merry.

**весе́лье**, rejoicing, merriment.

**весна́**, spring.

**весь, вся, всё, все,** all.

**ве́тер** (ве́тра), wind.

**ветеро́к**, breeze.

**ве́чер** (pl. вечера́), evening.

**ве́шать, пове́сить** (пове́шу, -ве́сишь), to hang, hang up.

**вещь** (f.), thing.

**взбира́ться, взобра́ться** (взберу́сь, -ёшься), to climb up, ascend.

**взволнова́ть.** (See **волнова́ть**.)

**вздыха́ть, вздохну́ть**, to sigh.

**взма́хивать, взмахну́ть**, to flap (wings).

**взор**, glance.

**взро́слый**, grown-up, adult.

**взять.** (See **брать**.)

**вид**, view, aspect.

**вида́ть, у-** (used only in infin. or past), to see.

**ви́деть, у-** (ви́жу, ви́дишь), to see.

**видне́ться, за-** (3rd person only), to be visible, appear.

**ви́дно**, apparently, it seems.

**ви́лка**, fork.

**висе́ть, по-** (вишу́, виси́шь), to hang (intrans.).

**вишнёвый**, cherry (adj.).

**вку́сный**, tasty.

**влеза́ть, влезть** (see **лезть**), to climb into, on to.

**вме́сте** (с + instr.), together (with).

**вме́сто** (gen.), instead of.

**вне** (gen.), out of, beyond.

**вниз**, down, downstairs, below (motion).

**внизу́**, down, downstairs, below (rest).

**вну́тренний**, inner, interior.

**вода́** (acc. во́ду, pl. во́ды), water.

**во́дка**, vodka.

**возвраща́ться, возврати́ться** (возвращу́сь, -ти́шься), or **верну́ться**, to return.

во́здух, air.
возмо́жность (f.), possibility, opportunity.
во́зраст, age.
вокру́г (gen.), round.
во́лжский, Volga (adj.).
волк, wolf.
волна́, wave.
волнова́ть, вз-, за- (волну́ю, -у́ешь), to agitate, excite.
вопро́с, question.
воро́та (nom. plur.), gates, gateway.
воротни́к, collar.
во́семь, eight.
восто́к, East.
восто́рг, enthusiasm.
вот, here is, here are.
впада́ть, впасть (впаду́, -ёшь; past: впал, впа́ла, -и), to flow into.
впаде́ние, mouth of a river.
вперёд, ahead, on.
впереди́, in front.
вре́мя (gen. вре́мени, pl. времена́), time.
во вре́мя (gen.), during.
во́ время, in good time, at the right time.
всё (adv.), continually, still, always.
всегда́, always.
вспо́мнить. (See по́мнить.)
встава́ть (встаю́, -ёшь), встать (вста́ну, -ешь), to get up, stand up.
встреча́ть, встре́тить (встре́чу, встре́тишь), to meet.
вся́кий, (pron.) everyone; (adj.) every.
второ́й, second.
вход, entrance.
входи́ть, войти́ (see ходи́ть and идти́), to enter.
выбира́ть, вы́брать (-беру -ешь), to choose.

выгля́дывать, вы́глянуть, to look out.
выде́лывать, вы́делать, to do, make, manufacture.
выку́ривать, вы́курить, to smoke (to the end).
вылеза́ть, вы́лезть (see лезть), to climb out.
вылива́ть, вы́лить (see лить), to pour out.
вынима́ть, вы́нуть, to take out.
вы́нырнуть, pf., to emerge.
выпива́ть, вы́пить (see пить), to drink up.
выпуска́ть, вы́пустить (-пущу, -пустишь), to let go.
выраже́ние, expression.
высо́кий (compar. вы́ше, superl. высоча́йший), high, tall.
вытя́гивать, вы́тянуть, to draw out, pull out, stretch out.
выходи́ть, вы́йти (see ходи́ть and идти́), to go out, come out.
вы́ше. (See высо́кий.)
вя́заный, knitted.


## Г

гада́ть, у-, to guess.
га́лстук, tie.
где, where.
где-нибу́дь, anywhere.
глава́, chapter.
гла́вный, chief, principal (adj.).
глаз (nom. plur. глаза́, gen. глаз), eye.
глубо́кий (compar. глу́бже), deep.
глу́пый, stupid.
гляде́ть, по- (гляжу́, гляди́шь), to look.
гля́нец, gloss, glaze.
говори́ть, по-, сказа́ть (q.v.), to speak, talk, say, tell.
годи́ть, по-, to wait a little.
голова́, голо́вка, head.

голо́дный, hungry.
го́лос (pl. голоса́), voice.
голубо́й, sky-blue.
голу́бчик, my dear.
гора́ (pl. го́ры), mountain.
го́рбить, с- (-блю, -бишь), to bend, arch.
гори́стый, mountainous.
го́род (pl. города́), town, city.
горя́чий, hot, burning.
гости́ная, drawing-room, sitting-room.
гость (m.), guest.
госуда́рство, state.
гото́вый, ready.
гото́вить, при- (-влю, -вишь), to prepare.
грамма́тика, grammar.
грани́ца, frontier.
гроза́, thunderstorm.
гром, thunder.
грома́дный, huge.
гро́мкий (compar. гро́мче), loud.
грудь (f.), breast.
грузови́к, lorry.
гря́зный, dirty, soiled.
гуля́ть, по-, to go for a walk.
густо́й, thick.


### Д

да, yes, and.
дава́ть (даю́, даёшь), дать (дам, дашь, даст, дади́м, дади́те, даду́т) to give, allow, let.
давно́, long ago, for a long time.
да́же, even.
далеко́ (also далёко), far.
да́льше (comp. of above), farther.
да́ча, country-house, villa.
да́чный, country (adj.).
два, две (f.), two.
два́дцать, twenty.
двенадцатиле́тний, twelve-year-old.

дви́гать, дви́нуть, to move.
двор, court, courtyard.
дворе́, на, outside, out-of-doors.
двухэта́жный, two-storied, two-decker.
де́вочка, little girl.
дежу́рить, по-, to be on duty.
де́йствие, act, action.
де́лать, с-, to do, make.
день (gen. дня, etc.), day.
де́ньги (gen. де́нег) (pl. only), money.
де́рево (nom. pl. дере́вья, gen. дере́вьев), tree.
дере́вня, country, village.
деревя́нный, wooden, timber (adj.).
держа́ть, по- (держу́, де́ржишь), to hold, keep.
де́сять, ten.
де́ти (gen. дете́й), children.
де́тская, nursery.
де́тство, childhood.
дива́н, sofa, divan.
ди́кий, wild.
длина́, length.
дли́ться, про- (3rd person only), to last.
для (gen.), for.
до (gen.), until, up to.
добира́ться, добра́ться (-беру́сь, -берёшься), to reach, attain.
дово́льный (instr.), pleased, content (with).
доезжа́ть, дое́хать (-е́ду, -е́дешь), to ride to, reach.
дождь (m.), rain, shower.
до́ктор (pl. доктора́), doctor.
до́лгий, long.
до́лжен, должна́, -но́, -ны́, must.
дом (pl. дома́), house.
до́ма, at home.
дома́шний, domestic.
домо́вый, house (adj.).
домо́й, home(-wards).

доноси́ться, донести́сь (see носи́ть and нести́), to be carried (up to), to reach.
доро́га, road.
дорого́й, dear.
достава́ть (-стаю́, -стаёшь), доста́ть, (-ста́ну, -ста́нешь), to secure, reach, get hold of, obtain.
доста́точно, enough.
дочу́рка (dimin. of дочь), (little) daughter.
дочь (до́чери, до́черью, pl. до́чери), daughter.
дразни́ть, по-, to tease, mock.
дре́вний, ancient.
дрова́, logs, firewood.
друго́й, other.
ду́мать, по-, to think.
дуть, по-, to blow.
дух, spirit.
духота́, stuffiness.
ду́шный, stuffy, sultry.
дыша́ть, по- (дышу́, ды́шишь), to breathe.

## Е

его́, him, his.
её, her.
ежего́дный, yearly, annual.
е́здить (е́зжу, е́здишь), пое́хать (-е́ду, -е́дешь), to ride, drive, travel.
е́сли, if.
есть, съ- (ем, ешь, ест, еди́м, еди́те, едя́т; past: ел, е́ла, е́ли), to eat.
е́хать, по- (е́ду, е́дешь), to go (by conveyance).
ещё, still, yet, more, again.

## Ж

жар, жара́, heat.

жа́ркий, hot (of weather).
жасми́н, jasmine.
ждать, подо- (жду, ждёшь) + gen. to wait (for).
же, ж, but; emphasises preceding word.
желе́зная доро́га, railway.
желе́зный, iron (adj.).
жена́ (pl. жёны), affectionate form: жёнушка, wife.
жи́во, quickly, in lively fashion.
живопи́сный, picturesque.
живо́т, stomach.
жигулёвский, Zhiguli (adj.).
жизнь, life.
жить, про- (живу́, -ёшь), to live.
журча́ть, за- (журчу́, -чи́шь), to gurgle, ripple.

## З

за (acc., instr.), for, after, behind, beyond, at.
забавля́ть, заба́вить (-а́влю, -а́вишь), to amuse, entertain.
забеле́ться. (See беле́ться.)
заблесте́ть. (See блесте́ть.)
забыва́ть, забы́ть (забу́ду, -бу́дешь), to forget.
заведе́ние, establishment.
заволнова́ться. (See волнова́ться.)
за́втра, to-morrow.
за́втрак, breakfast, lunch.
за́втракать, по-, to have breakfast, lunch.
задава́ть, зада́ть (see дава́ть), to set, ask (question).
за́дний, back, rear (adj.).
заки́дывать, заки́нуть, to throw.
закрича́ть. (See крича́ть.)
закрыва́ть, закры́ть (-кро́ю, -кро́ешь), to close, cover.

**заку́ривать, закури́ть** (**-курю́, -ку́ришь**), to light (a pipe, cigarette, etc.).

**за́ла,** hall (dining, concert, etc.).

**замерза́ть, замёрзнуть,** to freeze, be frozen.

**замеча́тельный,** remarkable.

**замира́ть, замере́ть** (**-мру́, -мрёшь;** past: **за́мер, -ла, -ли**), to grow numb, sink, stop (of heart).

**занаве́ска,** curtain.

**запа́с,** stock, store.

**за́пах,** smell, scent.

**запо́мнить.** (See **по́мнить.**)

**заря́,** dawn, day-break.

**заседа́ние,** meeting, session.

**заслы́шать.** (See **слы́шать.**)

**застава́ть** (**застаю́, -ёшь**), **заста́ть** (**заста́ну, -ешь**), to surprise, overtake.

**застрели́ть.** (See **стреля́ть.**)

**затиха́ть, зати́хнуть** (past: **зати́х, -ла, -ли**), to grow still, cease.

**затопи́ть.** (See **топи́ть.**)

**затрудне́ние,** difficulty.

**заходи́ть, зайти́** (see **ходи́ть, итти́**), to come up, call.

**захоте́ть.** (See **хоте́ть.**)

**зацепля́ть, зацепи́ть** (**-плю, -це́пишь**), to hook.

**зачём,** why.

**зашата́ться.** (See **шата́ться.**)

**зашуме́ть.** (See **шуме́ть.**)

**звать, по-** (**зову́, зовёшь**), to call.

**звезда́** (pl. **звёзды**), star.

**звене́ть, за-** (**звеню́, звени́шь**), to sound.

**зда́ние,** building.

**здесь,** here.

**здоро́вый,** healthy, well.

**здра́вствуй(те),** how do you do? good morning, etc.

**земля́,** earth, land, ground.

**земляни́ка,** strawberry.

**зигза́г,** zigzag.

**зима́,** winter.

**знамени́тый,** famous.

**знать, у-,** to know.

**зна́чить** (impf. only), to mean.

**золото́й,** golden, gold (adj.).

**зуб,** tooth.

**зя́бнуть, о-,** to be chilled.

## И

**игра́,** game.

**игра́ть, сыгра́ть,** to play.

**идти́, итти́,** (**иду́, идёшь;** past: **шёл, шла́, шли́**), pf. **пойти́,** to go (on foot).

**из, и́зо** (gen.), out of, from.

**из-за** (gen.), from behind, from beyond, because of.

**из-под** (gen.), from under.

**изве́стный,** (well-) known.

**изорва́ть.** (See **рвать.**)

**и́зредка,** now and then.

**и́ли,** or.

**име́ть,** to have.

**и́мя** (gen. **и́мени,** pl. **имена́**), (Christian) name.

**и́наче,** otherwise.

**иногда́,** sometimes.

**интере́сный,** interesting.

**иска́ть, по-** (**ищу́, и́щешь**) and gen., look for.

**испуга́ться.** (See **пуга́ться.**)

**исто́рия,** history, story.

**их,** them, their.

**ию́ль** (m.), July.

**ию́нь** (m.), June.

## К

**к, ко** (dat.), to, towards.

**кавка́зец** (gen. **-а́зца**), Caucasian.

**ка́ждый,** each, every.

**каза́ться, по-** (**кажу́сь, ка́жешься**) to seem, appear.

как, how, as, when.
как бу́дто, как бы, as if.
как . . . так и, both . . . and.
как то́лько, as soon as.
како́в, како́й, what, what kind of.
како́й-нибу́дь, some, any.
кали́тка, side-gate, wicket-gate.
калмы́к, Kalmuck.
ка́менный, stone (adj.), stony.
кани́кулы, holidays.
капита́н, captain.
капита́нский, adj. to above.
капу́ста, cabbage.
карма́н, pocket.
ка́рточный, card- (adj.).
каспи́йский, Caspian.
ката́ться, по-, to drive, go (car, skates, etc.).
Ка́тя (dim. of Катери́на), Kate.
кача́ть, по- (пока́чивать, frequentative), to rock.
кача́ть голово́й, по-, to shake one's head.
ка́чество, quality.
каю́та, cabin.
кварти́ра, flat.
квартира́нт, occupant of flat, lodger.
квас, kvass (kind of rye cider).
кипе́ть, за- (киплю́, -пи́шь), to boil.
кирги́з, Kirghiz.
кирпи́ч, brick.
кисе́йный, muslin.
класс, class.
класть (кладу́, -дёшь), положи́ть (положу́, -ло́жишь), to put (flat), lay.
клу́мба, flower-bed.
кни́га, book.
кни́зу, downwards.
ковёр (gen. ковра́), carpet.
ковы́ль (m.), feather-grass.
когда́, when.
ко́е-что, something.

колыха́ть, колыхну́ть, to shake, rock, ruffle.
комите́т, committee.
ко́мната, room.
комо́д, chest of drawers.
коне́ц (gen. конца́), end.
коне́чно, of course.
констру́кция, construction.
конце́рт, concert.
конча́ть, ко́нчить, to finish.
коню́шня, stable.
кора́бль (m.), ship.
корзи́на, dimin. корзи́ночка, basket.
корма́, stern (of ship).
корми́ть, на- (кормлю́, ко́рмишь), to feed.
коро́бка, box.
коро́ткий, short.
ко́рчиться, с-, to make faces.
костю́м, suit, costume.
котёнок (gen. котёнка, pl. котя́та) kitten.
кото́рый, who, which.
котя́та, pl. of котёнок.
ко́фточка, woman's jacket.
кошелёк (gen. кошелька́), purse.
ко́шка, cat.
край (pl. края́), border, edge, end.
краси́вый, beautiful.
кра́сненький, nice red.
красне́ть, по-, to grow red, blush.
кра́сный, red.
красота́, beauty.
кремль (m.), Kremlin, citadel.
кре́сло, arm-chair.
крестья́нка, peasant-girl or woman.
крик, cry, shout.
крича́ть, за- (кричу́, -чи́шь), кри́кнуть, to cry, shout.
крова́ть (f.), bed.
кро́ме (gen.), besides.
круго́м (gen.), round, around.
кру́пный, big, sturdy.
круто́й, steep, craggy.

крыло́ (nom. pl. кры́лья, gen. кры́льев), wing.
кры́ша, roof.
кто, who.
кто-нибу́дь, someone, anyone.
кто-то, someone.
кувши́н, pitcher.
куда́, where, whither.
купа́ть(ся), вы-, to bathe.
купе́ц (gen. купца́), merchant.
купи́ть. (See покупа́ть.)
ку́ртка, jacket.
куст, bush, shrub.
куха́рка, cook.
ку́хня, kitchen.
ку́шанье, dish, food.
ку́шать, по-, to eat.


## Л

ла́мпа, lamp.
ла́па, ла́пка, paw.
ле́бедь (m.), swan.
лёгкий, light, easy.
лёд (gen. льда), ice.
лежа́ть, по- (лежу́, лежи́шь), to lie.
лезть, по- (ле́зу, ле́зешь; past: лез, -ла, -ли), to climb.
лес (pl. леса́), forest, wood.
леси́стый, wooded.
лесно́й, forest (adj.).
ле́стница, stair, ladder.
лете́ть, по- (лечу́, лети́шь), to fly. (be flying.)
ле́тний, summer (adj.).
ле́то, summer.
лётчик, airman, pilot.
лимо́н, lemon.
лить, по- (лью, льёшь), to pour.
ли́ться (as above), to flow.
ло́вкий, skilful.
ло́дка, boat.
луг (pl. луга́), meadow.
лука́, bend.

лу́чше, better.
льдом, instr. of лёд.
люби́мый, favourite.
люби́ть, по- (люблю́, лю́бишь), to like, love.
любова́ться, на (-бу́юсь, бу́ешься) + instr., to admire.
лю́ди (gen. люде́й), people.
люк, trap-door.


## М

магази́н, shop.
маку́шка, top.
ма́ленький, little.
мали́на, raspberry.
ма́льчик, boy.
ма́мочка, dimin. of ма́ма, mother, mummy.
мануфакту́рный, manufacturing.
матро́с, sailor, seaman.
мать, mother (see дочь).
маха́ть, махну́ть, to beat, flap.
ма́чта, mast.
ме́бель (f.), furniture, piece of furniture.
ме́жду (instr.), between.
ме́лочь (f.), small change.
ме́сто, place, seat.
ме́сяц, month, moon.
ме́сячный, of the moon.
меха́ника, mechanics.
ми́ленький, dearest, darling.
ми́лый, dear, nice.
ми́мо (gen.), past.
мину́та, minute.
мириа́ды, myriads.
мла́дший, younger.
мно́го (gen.), much, many.
мо́жет быть, perhaps.
мо́жно, it is possible, (one) may, can.
мой, моя́, моё, pl. мои́, my.
мо́лния, lightning.

молодёжь (f.), youth, young people.
молодéц (gen. молодцá), young man, fine fellow, good lad.
молодóй, young.
молокó, milk.
мóлча, in silence, silently.
молчáть, за- (молчý, -ишь), to be silent.
мóре, sea.
морóзный, frosty, icy.
Москвá, Moscow.
москóвский, adj. to above.
мостовáя, pavement.
мочь, с- (могý, мóжешь, мóгут; past: мог, моглá, -ли), to be able.
муж (pl. мужья, gen. мужéй), husband.
мысль (f.), thought, idea.
мыться, у- (мóюсь, мóешься), to wash.
мягкий, soft.
мясо, meat.
мяýкать, за-, to mew.

## Н

на (acc. and prep.), on, on to, to, for, till.
набегáть, набежáть (-бегý, -бежишь, -бегýт), to come up quickly.
набивáть, набить (пóгреб) (набью, -бьёшь), to fill with (pp. 41).
навéрно, certainly.
наверхý, upstairs.
нáвык, habit, practice.
над (instr.), over, above.
надевáть, надéть (надéну, -ешь), to put on (clothes).
нáдо, it is necessary.
назáд, back, backwards.
называть, назвáть (назовý, -ёшь), to call, name.

наконéц, at last.
накрывáть на стол, накрыть (-крóю, -крóешь), to lay the table.
налéво, to the left.
наполнять, напóлнить, to fill.
нарóд, people, nation.
нарóдность (f.), nationality.
нарушáть, нарýшить, to disturb.
наслаждáться, насладиться (наслаждýсь, насладишься) (instr.), to enjoy.
наслаждéние, enjoyment.
нá-спех, hastily.
находить, найти (see ходить and идти), to find.
начáло, beginning.
начинáть, начáть (начнý, -нёшь), to begin.
наш, нáша, нáше, pl. нáши, our.
нашёл, past tense of найти.
нéбо (pl. небесá), sky, heaven.
недалекó (also недалёко) от (gen.), close to, not far from.
недéля, week.
недóлгий, short.
нéжный, tender, delicate.
незабывáемый, unforgettable.
нельзя, it is impossible, (one) must not.
немнóго, немнóжко (gen.), a little, a few, few.
необходимый, necessary.
необыкновéнный, unusual.
непремéнно, without fail.
неприятный, unpleasant.
нéсколько (gen. or из + gen.), a few, several.
нет, no, there is not, are not.
нести, по- (несý, -сёшь; past: нёс, неслá, -ли), to carry (be carrying).
нигдé, nowhere.
ниже, compar. of низкий.
нижний, lower, under (adj.).
низкий, low.

низовой, lower down the river (adj.).

никогда, never.

никто, nobody.

ничто, ничего, nothing; never mind (ничего).

но, but.

новый, new.

нож, knife.

нос, nose.

носить (ношу, носишь), to carry (frequentative).

носок (gen. носка), sock.

ночь (f.), night.

нравиться, по- (нравлюсь, нравишься) + dat., to please.

ну!, well!

нужно, one has to, must.

нынешний, present, to-day's.

нырять, нырнуть, to dive.

## O

оба, обе (fem.), both.

обед, dinner.

обедать, по-, to have dinner.

обезьяна, monkey.

обивать, обить (обобью, -бьёшь), to upholster.

обильный, abundant, plentiful.

облако (gen. pl. облаков), dimin. облачко, cloud.

обогащать, обогатить (-щу, -тишь), to enrich.

обрадоваться. (See радоваться.)

образ, form.

образовать (impf. and pf.) (образую, -уешь), to form.

обходить, обойти (see ходить and идти), to go round.

общий, common, general.

объяснять, объяснить, to explain.

обыкновенно, usually.

обычный, usual, ordinary.

овальный, oval.

овощи (pl.; gen. овощей), vegetable.

огорчение, grief, sorrow.

один, одна, одно, одни, one, alone

однообразие, monotony.

озябнуть. (See зябнуть.)

оказываться, оказаться (-кажусь, -кажешься), to appear, prove.

оканчивать, окончить, to finish, complete.

окно (n. pl. окна, gen. окон), window.

около (gen.), near, about.

окончание, conclusion.

окончить. (See оканчивать.)

описание, description.

описывать, описать (-пишу, -пишешь), to describe.

опомниться (pf.), to recover, come to.

опускать, опустить (опущу, опустишь), to lower, drop.

опять, again.

орда, horde.

освежать, освежить, to freshen, cool.

освещать, осветить (-вещу, -ветишь), to light up, illuminate.

осень (f.), autumn.

ослабеть. (See слабеть.)

осматривать, осмотреть (-трю, -мотришь), to examine, inspect.

основывать, основать (осную, -уёшь), to found.

особенно, especially.

особенность (f.), peculiarity.

оставаться (остаюсь, остаёшься), остаться (останусь, -нешься), to remain, be left.

оставлять, оставить (-влю, -вишь), to leave.

остальной, remaining.

останавливать, остановить (-влю,
-новишь), to stop (trans.).
от (gen.), from.
отапливать, отопить (-плю,
-топишь), to heat.
ответ, answer.
отвечать, ответить (-вечу- -ве-
тишь), to answer.
отгонять, отогнать (отгоню,
-гонишь), to chase away.
отдалённый, distant.
отдельный, separate, individual.
отделять, отделить, to separate.
отдых, rest.
отдыхать, отдохнуть, to rest.
отец (gen. отца), father.
откладывать, отложить (-ложу,
-ложишь), to put off.
открывать, открыть (-крою,
-кроешь), to open.
откуда, from where.
отличие, distinction.
отлично, excellent(ly), very well.
отовсюду, from all parts.
отогнал. (See отгонять.)
отопить. (See отапливать.)
отопление, heating.
отполировать. (See полировать.)
отпуск, leave (of absence).
отражать, отразить (-ражу,
-разишь), to reflect.
отрог, spur (of mountain).
отрывать, оторвать (-рву,
-рвёшь), to tear away.
отставать (-стаю, -стаёшь), от-
стать (-стану, -станешь), to
lag behind, be slow (of clock).
отсылать, отослать (отошлю,
-шлёшь), to dispatch.
оттуда, from there.
отходить, отойти (see ходить and
идти), to depart, leave.
отчаяние, despair.
охотник, hunter.
очевидно, evidently.
очень, very.

**П**

падать (у)пасть (паду, падёшь,
past: пал, -ла, -ли), to fall.
палуба, deck.
папироса, cigarette.
пара, pair.
паркетный, parquet.
парной, warm, fresh (of milk).
пароход, steamer.
партийный, party (adj.).
пассажир, adj: пассажирский,
passenger.
пахнуть, за- (past: пах, -ла, -ли),
to smell.
пациент, patient.
пение, singing, song (of birds).
первый, first.
перед (instr.), before, in front of.
передняя, hall.
передразнивать, передразнить,
to mimic, mock.
перекладина, cross-beam, spar.
переменять, переменить, to
change.
передавать, передать (see давать),
to broadcast.
переодеваться, переодёться
(-денусь, -денешься), to change
(clothes).
переставать (-стаю, -стаёшь),
перестать (-стану, -станешь),
to stop, cease.
переулок (gen. переулка), lane,
by-street.
переходить, перейти (see ходить
and идти), to pass over, cross.
перс, Persian.
петля, loop.
печь (f.), stove.
пешеход, pedestrian.
пирожок (gen. sing. пирожка),
small tart.
писать, на- (пишу, пишешь), to
write.
пить, вы- (пью, пьёшь), to drink.

плáкать, за- (плáчу, плáчешь), to weep.

план, plan.

платúть, за- (плачý, плáтишь), to pay.

плáтье, dimin. плáтьице, dress.

плескáть (плещý, плéщешь), плеснýть (плеснý, плеснёшь), to splash.

плот, raft.

плохóй, bad.

плыть, по- (плывý, плывёшь), to sail.

по (dat.), by, along.

побóльше, a little larger or more.

пóвод, occasion.

по пóводу (gen.), apropos of.

погóда, weather.

погодúть. (See годúть.)

пóгреб (plur. погребá), cellar, ice-house.

под (acc., instr.), under.

подавáть, подáть (see давать), to give, give away, serve.

подáльше, a little further.

подбегáть, подбежáть (-бегý, -бежúшь), to run up (to).

пóдле (gen.), beside.

подмáнивать, подманúть, to beckon, entice.

поднимáть, поднять (-нимý, -нúмешь), to raise, lift up.

поднимáться, подняться (reflex. of above), to rise, go up.

подóбный, similar.

подпрýгивать, подпрýгнуть, to jump, skip up (to).

подскáкивать, подскакáть (-скачý -скáчешь), to gallop up (to).

подходящий, suitable.

подъéзд, approach, entrance to house.

пóезд (plur. поездá), train.

поéздка, excursion, trip.

позадú (gen.), behind.

пóздно, late.

покá, while; with fut. perf., until.

покá . . . не, until.

покáзывать, показáть (-кажý, -кáжешь), to show.

покáчивать. (See качáть.)

покрывáть, покрýть (-крóю, -крóешь), to cover.

покупáть, купúть (куплю́, кý-пишь), to buy.

покýпка, purchase; (in pl.) shopping.

пол, floor.

пóлдень (m.) (gen. полýдня) midday.

пóле, field.

полировáть, от- (-рýю, -рýешь), polish.

пóлка, shelf.

пóлный, full.

половúна, half.

полосá, stripe, band, streak.

полýдню. (See пóлдень.)

помéньше, a little smaller or less.

пóмнить, вс- or за-, to remember.

помогáть, помóчь (see мочь) (dat.), to help.

помóщница, assistant, helper.

понимáть, понять (поймý, поймёшь), to understand.

порá, it is time.

порядок (gen. порядка), order.

пóсле (gen.), after.

послéдний, last.

послýшаться. (See слýшаться.)

посредú, посредúне (gen.), in the middle (of).

пострóйка, building.

посýда, crockery.

потеплée, a little warmer.

потолóк (gen. потолкá), ceiling.

потóм, then, after that.

похóжий, similar.

почемý, why.

поэ́тому, so, therefore.

прáво, truly, I assure you.

пра́здник, holiday.

пра́чка, laundress.

предлага́ть, предложи́ть (-ложу́, -ло́жишь), to offer.

предназнача́ть, предназна́чить, to destine, fix.

предоставля́ть, предоста́вить (-влю, -вишь), to let, allow.

предпринима́ть, предприня́ть (-приму́, -при́мешь), to undertake.

пре́жде, formerly, before.

прекра́сный, beautiful, splendid.

прерыва́ть, прерва́ть (-рву́, -рвёшь), to interrupt, disturb.

при (prep.), by, near, at the time of.

приближа́ться, прибли́зиться (-бли́жусь, -бли́зишься), to approach.

привести́. (See following.)

приводи́ть (-вожу́, -во́дишь), привести́ (-веду́, -ведёшь; past: -вёл, -вела́, -вели́), to lead up (to), bring along.

приво́льный, abundant, fertile.

приду́мывать, приду́мать, to imagine, devise, invent.

приезжа́ть, прие́хать (-е́ду, е́дешь), to arrive (by conveyance).

прика́зчик, (shop) assistant.

прикла́дывать, приложи́ть (-ложу́, -ло́жишь), to add.

приложи́ть. (See above.)

приноси́ть, принести́ (see носи́ть and нести́), to bring.

приподнима́ться, приподня́ться (-нимусь, -ни́мешься) to rise.

приседа́ть, присе́сть (-ся́ду, -ся́дешь; past: сел, -ла, -ли). to squat, cower.

при́стань (f.), wharf, quay, landing-stage.

приходи́ть, прийти́ (see ходи́ть and идти́), to arrive.

прице́ливаться, прице́литься, to aim.

прия́тный, pleasant.

про́бовать, по- (-бую, -буешь), to try, test.

проводи́ть, провести́. (See приводи́ть) to spend (time).

програ́мма, programme.

продолжа́ть, продо́лжить, (trans.) to continue; (reflex.) to last.

продолже́ние, continuation.

проду́кт, product, produce, fruit.

прозра́чный, transparent.

промы́шленность (f.), industry.

проноси́ться, пронести́сь (see носи́ть and нести́), to blow hard, rush past.

проси́ть, по- (прошу́, про́сишь), to ask, beg.

пропада́ть, пропа́сть (see па́дать), to be lost.

просто́р, expanse.

просыпа́ться, просну́ться, to wake up.

противополо́жный, opposite.

прохла́дный, cool.

проходи́ть, пройти́ (see ходи́ть and идти́), to pass.

проче́сть. (See чита́ть.)

прочь, away, off.

пруд, pond.

пры́гать, пры́гнуть, to jump.

прыжо́к (gen. прыжка́), jump.

пря́мо, straight.

пти́чка (dimin. of пти́ца), little bird.

пуга́ться, ис-, to be frightened.

пу́динг, pudding.

пузы́рь (m.), bubble.

пуска́ть, пусти́ть (пущу́, пу́стишь), to let go, allow.

пуска́ться, пусти́ться (as above), to set off, plunge.

путеше́ствие, journey.

путеше́ствовать (-вую, -вуешь), по-, to travel.

пу́шечный, cannon (adj.).
пуши́стый, downy.
пы́льный, dusty.
пя́тый, fifth.
пять, five.
пятьдеся́т, fifty.

**Р**

рабо́та, work.
рабо́тать, по-, to work.
рабо́чий, working.
рад, ра́да, ра́ды, glad.
ра́дио (indecl.), radio.
ра́доваться, об- (ра́дуюсь, ра́ду-
 ешься), to be glad, enjoy oneself.
ра́дость (f.), joy.
раз (gen. pl. раз), time, occasion ;
 (advb.) once ; one (in counting).
разбуди́ть. (See буди́ть.)
развлече́ние, amusement, recrea-
 tion.
разгово́р, conversation.
раздава́ть, разда́ть (see дава́ть),
 to give away.
раздава́ться, разда́ться (impersonal), to be heard, sound.
раздева́ться, разде́ться (-де́нусь,
 -де́нешься), to undress, take
 one's things off.
разлива́ть, разли́ть (разолью́,
 -льёшь), to shed, diffuse.
разложи́ть. (See раскла́дывать.)
ра́нний, early.
ра́но, early, soon.
ра́ньше, earlier, before (advb.).
раскла́дывать, разложи́ть (-ложу́,
 -ло́жишь), to spread.
распла́каться (pf.) (-пла́чусь,
 -пла́чешься), to burst into tears.
распла́чиваться, расплати́ться
 (see плати́ть), to pay off, settle.
распуска́ть, распусти́ть (see
 пуска́ть) to let go, spread
 (wings).

расса́живаться, рассе́сться (see
 сади́ться), to sit down comfortably.
рассерди́ться. (See серди́ться.)
рассе́сться. (See расса́живаться.)
рассе́янный, absent-minded.
расска́з, tale, story.
расска́зывать, рассказа́ть (-скажу́,
 -ска́жешь), to tell, relate.
рассма́тривать, рассмотре́ть
 (-смотрю́, -смо́тришь), to dis-
 cern.
расти́, вы́расти (расту́, растёшь;
 past : рос, росла́, росли́), to grow.
рвать, изорва́ть (рву, рвёшь), to
 tear.
револю́ция, revolution.
река́, river.
рестора́н, restaurant.
ре́чка, brook, stream.
речь (f.), speech.
реша́ть, реши́ть, to decide.
ро́вный, even, level.
роди́ться. (See рожда́ться.)
ро́жа (f.), (slang) phiz, face.
рожда́ться, роди́ться, to be born.
рос. (See расти́.)
Росси́я, Russia.
рот (gen. рта), mouth.
роя́ль (m.), grand piano.
руба́шка, shirt.
ружьё, rifle.
рука́ (acc. ру́ку, pl. ру́ки), arm,
 hand.
ру́сский, Russian.
ры́ба, fish.
ры́бный, fish (adj.).
ры́нок (gen. ры́нка), market.
рю́мка, dimin. рю́мочка, wine-
 glass.
ря́дом, side by side, next door.

**С**

с, со, (with instr.) with ; (with
 gen.) from, off.

сад, garden. N.B. в саду́.

сади́ться (сажу́сь, сади́шься), сесть (ся́ду, -ешь; past. сел, -а, -и), to sit down.

сала́т, salad, lettuce.

салфе́тка, serviette, table-napkin.

сам, self, oneself.

сама́рский, of Samara.

самова́р, samovar.

самолёт, aeroplane.

са́мый, very, most (used to form superlative).

сара́й, shed, coach-house.

све́жесть (f.), freshness, coolness.

свежѣ́ть, по-, to become fresh, cool.

све́жий, fresh, cool.

сверка́ть, сверкну́ть, to flash.

свет (no plural), light, world.

све́тлый, bright, clear.

свобо́да, freedom.

свобо́дный, free.

свози́ть (свожу́, -во́зишь), свезти́ (свезу́, -ёшь; past: -вёз, -везла́, -ли́), to convey, carry, transport.

свой, one's own.

себя́, self, oneself.

сего́дня, to-day.

сейча́с, presently; with же, at once.

секу́нда, second.

семе́йный, family (adj.).

семна́дцать, seventeen.

семь, seven.

семья́, (gen. pl. семе́й), family.

се́ни (f. pl.; gen. сене́й), entrance-hall.

сентя́брь (m.), September.

серди́ться, рас- (сержу́сь, се́рдишься), to be angry.

серебро́, silver.

середи́на, middle.

се́рый, grey.

сестра́ (nom. pl. сёстры, gen. сестёр), sister.

се́тка, gauze, film.

сза́ди (gen.), behind, from behind.

Сиби́рь (f.), Siberia.

сиде́ть, по- (сижу́, сиди́шь), to sit, be sitting.

си́ла, strength, force.

си́льный, strong.

симфони́ческий, symphony (adj.).

синѣ́ть, по-, to become, appear blue.

си́ний, blue.

сире́нь (f.), lilac.

сказа́ть (perfective of говори́ть) (скажу́, ска́жешь), to say, tell.

скака́ть, по- (скачу́, ска́чешь), to gallop.

скали́стый, rocky.

скаме́йка, bench.

скидывать, ски́нуть, to throw down or off, pull off.

скла́дывать, сложи́ть (сложу́, сло́жишь), to fold.

ско́лько (gen.), how much, how many.

ско́рый, quick.

скрыва́ться, скры́ться (скро́юсь, -ешься), to disappear.

слабѣ́ть, о-, to grow weak.

сла́бый, weak, feeble.

сла́дкий, sweet.

сле́дующий, following, next.

слива́ться, сли́ться (see лить), to flow together, join (of rivers).

слова́рь, dictionary, vocabulary.

сло́во, word.

слу́жащий, employee, one serving.

слу́жба, service, work, office; (in pl.) out-houses.

служе́бная столо́вая, office canteen.

служи́ть, по-, to serve, work.

случа́ться, случи́ться (impersonal), to happen.

слу́шать, по-, to listen to.

слу́шаться, по-, to obey.

слы́шать, у- (слы́шу, -ишь), to hear; with perfective за-, to smell (transitive).
слы́шный, audible.
смесь (f.), medley, mixture.
смешно́й, funny.
сморо́дина, currant.
смотре́ть, по- (смотрю́, смо́тришь), to look.
смотря́ по (dat.), according to.
смочь. (See мочь.)
снару́жи (gen.), outside.
снима́ть, снять (сниму́, сни́мешь), to take off.
сно́ва, again, anew.
снять. (See снима́ть.)
соба́ка, dog, hound.
собира́ть, собра́ть (соберу́, -ёшь), to collect, gather; (reflex. + infin.) to be on the point of doing something.
собра́ние, meeting.
со́бственный, own.
совреме́нный, contemporary.
совсе́м, quite.
соединя́ть, соедини́ть, to unite, join.
сожале́нию, к, unfortunately.
со́лнце, sun.
солове́й (gen. соловья́), nightingale.
со́рок, forty.
сосе́дний, neighbouring.
сосно́вый, pine (adj.).
составля́ть, соста́вить (-влю, -вишь), to compose.
со́ус, sauce.
сохрани́ть. (See храни́ть.)
сохраня́ться, сохрани́ться, to last
сочине́ние, essay.
спаса́ть, спасти́ (-су́, -сёшь; past : спас, -ла́, -ли́), to save.
спаси́тель, saviour.
спать, по- (сплю, спишь), to sleep.
спекта́кль (m.), play.
специа́льный, special.

спеши́ть, по-, to hurry.
спех, hurry, haste.
спина́, back.
сплошь, continuously.
споко́йный, calm.
спра́шивать, спроси́ть (спрошу́, спро́сишь), to ask.
спры́гивать, спры́гнуть, to jump off, from.
спуска́ться, спусти́ться (спущу́сь, спу́стишься), to come down, fall.
сра́внивать, сравни́ть, to compare.
сра́зу, all at once.
среди́ (gen.), among
сре́дний, middle (adj.).
срыва́ть, сорва́ть (сорву́, сорвёшь), to tear off, away.
ста́вить, по- (ста́влю, ста́вишь), to put (upright), produce on stage.
ста́вня, shutter.
ста́до, herd, flock.
стака́н, glass, tumbler.
станови́ться (-влю́сь, -бвишься), стать (ста́ну, ста́нешь), to stand up, become; perf. form also = to begin.
стара́ться, по-, to try.
старина́, old times.
стари́нный, ancient.
ста́рший, elder.
ста́рый, old.
стать. (See станови́ться.)
стекля́нный, glass (adj.).
стена́, wall.
степь (f.), steppe.
стол, dimin. сто́лик, table.
столе́тие, century.
столо́вая, dining-room.
сторона́, side, direction.
стоя́ть, по- (стою́, стои́шь), to stand.
страна́, country, land.
страх, fear, anxiety.
стреля́ть, по-, also застрели́ть, to shoot.
стро́ить, по-, to build.

студе́нтка, girl-student.

стул (nom. pl. сту́лья, gen. сту́льев), chair.

ступа́ть, ступи́ть (ступлю́, сту́пишь), to step, walk.

суме́ть. (See уме́ть.)

су́мка, bag.

су́тки (pl. only), 24 hours.

сухо́й, compar. су́ше, dry.

существова́ть, про- (-ву́ю, -ву́ешь)- to exist.

схва́тывать, схвати́ть (схвачу́, схва́тишь) to catch, seize.

сходи́ть, сойти́ (see ходи́ть and идти́), to come down, off.

счастли́вый, happy.

сча́стью, к, fortunately.

сын (nom. pl. сыновья́, gen. сынове́й), son.

съеда́ть, съесть (see есть), to eat (up).

съезжа́ться, съе́хаться (-е́дусь, -е́дешься), to assemble.

сюда́, here, hither.

## Т

т.е. = то есть, i.e.

таи́нственный, mysterious.

та́йный, secret.

так, so.

так как, as, since.

та́кже, also.

таки́м о́бразом, so, in that way.

тако́й, such.

там, there.

та́нец (gen. та́нца), dance.

танцова́ть, по (танцу́ю, -у́ешь), to dance.

таре́лка, plate.

тата́рин (nom. pl. тата́ры, gen. тата́р, Tatar, Tartar.

твой, thy, your.

теа́тр, theatre.

те́ло, body.

теля́тина, veal.

темне́ть, по-, to grow dark.

тёмно-си́ний, dark-blue.

тени́стый, shady.

тень (f.), shade.

тепло́ (noun), warmth.

тёплый, adv. тепло́, warm.

тётя, aunt.

течь, по- (теку́, течёшь; past: тёк, текла́, -ли́), to flow.

ти́хий, calm, quiet.

тишина́, quiet, stillness, silence.

то . . . то, now . . . now.

това́рищ, comrade, companion.

тогда́, then, at that time.

то́же, also.

то́лстый, thick.

то́лько, only.

то́лько что, just, only just.

то́нкий, thin, shrill.

топи́ть за- (топлю́, то́пишь), to heat.

тот, та, то, те, that.

тот-же, the same.

то́тчас-же (also тотча́с), at once.

трава́, grass.

трамва́й, tram.

тре́тий, -тья, -тье, third.

тро́е (gen.), three persons, things.

тру́дный, difficult.

трюм, hold.

туда́, thither, there.

ту́ча, dimin. ту́чка, thunder-cloud.

тяжёлый, heavy.

## У

у (gen.), at, by.

убега́ть, убежа́ть (-бегу́, -бежи́шь), to run away, escape.

увели́чивать, увели́чить, to increase.

уга́дывать, угада́ть, to guess.

у́гол (gen. угла́; в, на углу́), corner.

удава́ться, уда́ться (see дава́ть), (impers. + dat.) to succeed.
удиви́тельный, wonderful.
удивле́ние, surprise.
уди́ть, по- (ужу́, у́дишь), to angle, fish.
удо́бный, comfortable.
удово́льствие, pleasure.
уезжа́ть, уе́хать (-е́ду, -е́дешь), to go away.
уж, уже́, already.
ужа́сно, frightfully.
у́жинать, по-, to have supper.
улета́ть, улете́ть (-лечу́, -лети́шь) to fly away.
у́лица, street.
умеря́ть, уме́рить, to moderate, temper.
уме́ть, с-, to know how to, be able.
универса́льный, universal.
университе́т, university.
упа́сть. (See па́дать.)
употребля́ть, употреби́ть (-блю́, -би́шь), to use.
ура́льский, Ural (adj.).
уро́к, lesson.
уса́живаться, усе́сться (-ся́дусь, -ешься), to take a seat.
услы́шать. (See слы́шать.)
успева́ть, успе́ть, to have time.
успока́ивать, успоко́ить, to reassure, set at ease.
устава́ть, уста́ть (like встава́ть), to get tired.
устра́ивать, устро́ить, to arrange.
уступа́ть, -пи́ть (-ступлю́, -сту́пишь), to give way.
у́тро, (adj.) у́тренний, morning.
уходи́ть, уйти́ (see ходи́ть and идти́), to go away, leave.
учени́к, pupil.
учи́тель (nom. pl. -ля́), teacher.
учи́тельница, fem. of above.
учи́ться, вы-, to study, learn.
ую́тный, snug, comfortable.

**Ф**

фа́брика, factory.
фарфо́р, china, porcelain.
флане́левый, flannel (adj.).
фра́за, phrase, sentence.
францу́зский, French.

**Х**

ходи́ть, по- (хожу́, хо́дишь), to go (on foot).
хозя́ин (pl. хозя́ева), master, proprietor.
хо́лод, cold.
холо́дный, advb. хо́лодно, cold.
хоро́ший, advb. хорошо́, good, fine.
хоте́ть, за- (хочу́, хо́чешь, хоти́м, хотя́т), to want.
храни́ть, со-, to keep.
хруста́льный, crystal.
ху́же (comp. of плохо́й), worse.

**Ц**

цвето́к (gen. цветка́, pl. цветы́), flower.
центр, adj. центра́льный, centre.
цепля́ть, зацепи́ть, to hook, catch hold of, brush against.
це́рковь (gen. це́ркви, instr. це́рковью), church.

**Ч**

ча́ек. (See ча́йка.)
чай, tea.
ча́йка, sea-gull.
час, hour.
ча́стый, advb. ча́сто, frequent.
часть (f.), part.
ча́ще, more often.

человѣ́к (pl. лю́ди), man, person.
чем, than.
че́рез (acc.), over, across, through, in.
черта́, line, mark.
четве́рг, Thursday.
четы́ре, four.
число́, number.
чи́стый, clean.
чита́ть, про-, or проче́сть (-чту́, -ёшь, past : -чёл, -чла́, -чли́), to read.
чи́ще, cleaner.
член, member.
что, что̀, that, what, which (conj.)
что́бы, in order to, in order that.
что за, what kind of.
что́-то, что-нибу́дь, something.
чу́вствовать, по- (чу́вствую, -ешь), to feel.
чуде́сный, marvellous.
чуло́к (gen. чулка́), stocking.
чуть, almost, scarcely.
чуть не, very nearly.

шу́ба, fur-coat.
шум, noise.
шумѣ́ть, за-, to make a noise.

## Щ

щи (pl. only ; gen. щей), cabbage-soup.

## Э

экза́мен, examination.
экипа́ж, carriage (horse-drawn).
элева́тор, elevator.
эпизо́д, episode.
эта́ж, storey, floor.
э́тот, э́та, э́то, э́ти, this.

## Ю

ю́бка, skirt.

## Ш

шата́ться, за-, to stagger.
шевели́ть, по-, to move, stir.
шесть, six.
ше́я, (gen. pl. шей) neck.
шипо́вник, wild rose.
широ́кий, compar. ши́ре, wide.
шкаф, cupboard.
шко́ла, school.
шля́па, hat.
што́ра, blind.
штоф, silk stuff, damask.

## Я

явля́ться, яви́ться (явлю́сь, я́вишься), to appear.
я́года, berry.
ядро́, bullet.
язы́к, tongue, language.
яи́чный, adj. of яйцо́, egg.
я́ма, pit, hole.
я́ркий, bright.
я́рмарка, fair.
я́рче, compar. of я́ркий.
я́щик, drawer, box.